LORD KILDARE'S GRAND TOUR

Elizabeth FitzGerald was a daughter of Major Charles Fleetwood-
Hesketh of Stockton Hall, Rutland (England).
In 1936 she married Brian FitzGerald,
a direct descendant of Kildare, who wrote a number of books
on the FitzGeralds. In helping him Elizabeth realised
there was an interesting story to tell about
Lord Kildare's Grand Tour. She researched 'Grand Tours'
generally and wrote a background narrative for Kildare's letters.
After Elizabeth's death in 1991, her brother-in-law,
Denis FitzGerald, showed her typescript to Molly Keane
who wrote a foreword just before her death.

Lord Kildare's Grand Tour
The Letters of William FitzGerald 1766-1769

Elizabeth FitzGerald

The Collins Press

PUBLISHED BY
The Collins Press, West Link Park, Doughcloyne, Wilton, Cork, 2000

© Elizabeth FitzGerald

British Library Cataloguing in Publication data.

ISBN: 1-898256-78-0

Printed in Ireland by Betaprint

Jacket design by Upper Case Ltd.

CONTENTS

PREFACE

The FitzGeralds were the pre-eminent Irish gentry family, used to taking their place as the leaders of Irish opinion, fashion and politics. As long ago as Giraldus Cambrensis, they had been heeded as the bulwark of the colony:

> Who are the men who penetrate the enemy's innermost strongholds? The FitzGeralds. Who are the men who protect their native land? The FitzGeralds. Who are the men the enemy fear? The FitzGeralds. Who are the men who envy denigrates? The FitzGeralds.

By the late Middle Ages, they routinely ran the colony, and even when their power was broken in the early modern period, they still assumed that they were the oldest, most prestigious and therefore premier Irish aristocratic family. They were also closely allied to the Duke of Goodwood, leader of the powerful Lennox family in England.

For the young men of the FitzGeralds, therefore, the fashionable Grand Tour of Europe was a routine part of their education. This book chronicles the experience of William FitzGerald, later Duke of Leinster, on his tour between 1766 and 1769. William was the second son in a vast family and as such destined for a good commission in the army. His life changed dramatically when his eldest brother George died in 1765 and William was catapulted into a role for which he had not been prepared, and to which he was temperamentally unprepared – leader of a hugely influential political and cultural circle. As he was later to point out to his mother, he embraced this role only from a sense of duty:

> ... if I could at once see them [his brothers] all settled in their professions I believe I should myself give up all politics as I am not calculated for it. Indeed I should give myself very little trouble about it was it not a duty I owe my family.

The Grand Tour was hastily designed to add polish and finesse to this dull if decent young man – described as 'meek and obliging' by his Aunt Lady Holland, and of 'plain and decent appearance' by Charles Bentinck. Inclined to put on weight, slightly hypochondriac, maladroit (he trod on the toes of Italian ladies of Turin), William did his best to fit into his flamboyant family. He spent money on fashion, acquired trendy Italian prints, vases and flowers, took Italian and dancing lessons, and visited with the highest families in Italy and Austria.

All the while, he corresponded regularly with his formidable mother Emily, Duchess of Leinster, one of the most prolific letter writers of the eighteenth-century world. Indeed, the FitzGeralds, as William's own letters demonstrate, are the best-documented family of this period. The quality and range of this correspondence has been brilliantly demonstrated in Stella Tillyard's *Aristocrats* – also made into a BBC costume drama filmed in Ireland – which covers the intertwined lives of the four Lennox sisters – Caroline, Emily, Louisa and Sarah. Three of them ended up living in close proximity in Kildare in Carton (Emily), Castletown (Louisa) and Celbridge (Sarah). The vast array of letters from within this massive extended family offer an unrivalled perspective on family life in gentry circles in mid eighteenth-century Ireland. The act of writing and reading letters was social and performative; it was a daily routine for the FitzGeralds which held together a widely scattered dynasty in an intimately choreographed constellation. Letters implied recipro-city and a constant circuit of affection which maintained cohesion between the Irish and English based members. For Emily, letters were also a way of wielding her astonishing array of soft but formidable manipulative skills on her fractured family; she ruled as a loving doyenne long after the scattering of her children.

Traditionally letters have been valued by historians because they seem to offer unmediated access to their writers' true feelings. A close analysis of the FitzGerald letters caution against this hasty response. The vast bulk of these letters were never intended as priviledged communications; letters were routinely read aloud and passed on within the family circle; they occupied an intermediate space between public and private. They were never regarded as being equally intimate as a face-to-face conversation (these were highly prized by the FitzGerald children, especially with Emily in her boudoir).

George Moore, in *A Drama in Muslin*, claimed that in Ireland: 'during the winter months, the letters fell like rain and they were circulated like magazines.' In the FitzGerald circle, a constant stream of letters flowed between its principal nodes – Carton, Castletown and Celbridge in Kildare, Leinster House and Frescati in Dublin, Harley Street – their town residence in London – and Goodwood, seat of the acknowledged pinnacle of the family, the Duke of Richmond. The letters flowed overwhelmingly between the women and were sustaining in a psychological sense as a font of support, advice and intimacy. There is also a constant quest in these letters for news of fashion (it was important to the family that the younger FitzGeralds led the style in Dublin), furniture, décor (a constant query was what colours were fashionable in Paris and London), and reading (there are many lengthy responses to authors – Maria Edgeworth, Abbe Barruel, Madame de Genlis). William's letters from his Grand Tour fit into this rich circuit of news, gossip, shopping and mutual support.

Never a solid high-flyer, like his brother Edward, William was already wishing to be 'settled' as he travelled across Europe. Back home, he succeeded as Duke of Leinster in 1773. A year later, he married Aemilia St George – considered dull if dependable by William's sisters. The two retired into country life at Carton: William enjoyed hunting, agriculture and estate improvement much more than politics or entertaining, and he was considered a less than skilful politician. He died in 1804, five years after his beloved Aemilia, with whom he enjoyed a loving marriage.

The Grand Tour was an essential aspect of aristocratic life. William's letters offer us a detailed perspective on such a tour and add to our knowledge of this remarkable FitzGerald family.

KEVIN WHELAN
Smurfit Director of Keough-Notre Dame Centre,
Newman House, Dublin
September 2000

FOREWORD

These intimate family letters from the archives of the FitzGerald family are a rare and tantalising pleasure for the reader today. This is largely because from their earliest recorded date, 1739, they are written with style and in a sharp, clear language, as far removed from the beautiful English of the Book of Common Prayer as the dialogue of Oscar Wilde is distant from the lyrics of WB Yeats.

The majority of the letters in the collection were written by the young Lord Kildare to his mother, the 1st Duchess of Leinster, telling her of his fascinating experiences while making the Grand Tour between 1766 and 1769. His reception by celebrities is recorded with a sharp eye for a touch of scandal equal to any report on social deviations today.

When in Rome he spares her heavy descriptions of famous churches and picture galleries, but does not fail to record his approval of the decorous fashion in which Cardinals were able to combine celibacy with fornication. The Pope gave him a gracious reception and allowed him the honour of kissing his toe which he reassures his mother, smelled very sweet.

Every letter he writes during the three years of the Tour neglects the obvious; exchanging it for a surprising detail of some kind.

When in Vienna – although he comes from Ireland – he neglects any description of the Emperor's famous white horses and dwells instead on his brief sight of Marie Antoinette, aged thirteen, in the Imperial Opera box. For us, who know her whole story, the pathos behind this happy scene brings her tragic fate very close.

Unimpressed by all the gilt and marble on display at the Herculean Museum he askes only to be shown the kitchen furniture that had survived the Vesuvius eruptions. He sends his mother details of a small cooking pot lined with silver.

Such choice of details, with many others more serious, give early proof of the sense and sensibility which in later years were to make him the best-loved Landlord in Ireland; second only to his younger brother, Lord Edward FitzGerald, a leader of the 1798 Rebellion, and one of Ireland's best loved patriots and martyrs.

MOLLY KEANE
Ardmore, County Waterford
March 1994

INTRODUCTION

In the spring of 1749 the Earl and Countess of Kildare were in London, having taken a house in Arlington Place. Here, on 2 March, their second son was born. He was called William Robert, and he lived to become second Duke of Leinster. Years later Lady Fludyer wrote to his mother – '... do you remember how I held your knees in Arlington Street when you was in labour of his Lordship, and how I had on a great hoop, and my lappets down, just going to the Ridotto? How well I recollect that night, and when I came to the Ridotto, and told Col B Sandford, he would not believe me, as he had left you at eight o'clock. There's an old story for you ...' At his christening the Earl of Inchiquin and Viscount Hillsborough were his godfathers, and Lady Kildare's mother, the Duchess of Richmond, his godmother.

From the glimpses we catch of him through his mother's letters, William seems to have been an attractive boy. In August, 1750, when he was seventeen months old, his mother describes him as a 'sweet little child', but not so active as his elder brother, George, Lord Ophaly, who was a year older than William. But he was able to say several words and to walk alone; 'his little person' was fat, round, and white; he was very good natured, 'excessively passionate already, but puts his little mouth to kiss and be friends the very next minute'.

When he was seven, William and his brother Lord Ophaly went to a school at Wandsworth, of which Monsieur Pampellone, a Frenchman of some celebrity, was master. William's cousin, Charles James Fox, who was his own age, was already there. On their way to school the two FitzGerald boys went to Holland House, the home of their aunt, Lady Caroline Fox, wife of Henry Fox, who became first Lord Holland. Holland House, a fine red-brick Jacobean mansion surrounded by trees, was then still in the country, a short distance beyond Kensington Palace.

To their mother Lady Caroline wrote: 'I have the pleasure to inform my dear sister that the dear little boys arrived here yesterday at five o'clock in perfect good health ... They are going to school to-day, where their cousin Charles will be glad to see them, I'm sure ... William's beauty is a little hurt with the loss of his tooth. I pity you, dear siss, from my heart, being obliged to part with them, but I do think Wandsworth School is the best nursery for delicate children in the world.'

In 1757 Lady Kildare came over to England from her home at Carton, County Kildare. She took her two little boys, George and

William, aged nine and eight respectively, to stay at Goodwood with the Duke and Duchess of Richmond. The Duke was Lady Kildare's elder brother; he married Lady Mary Bruce, daughter of Lord Ailesbury.

On 27 May Lady Kildare wrote to her husband in Ireland, '... Everybody loves our boys. They are so good-humoured and lively; particularly William, who is dying of love for the Duchess of Richmond. He cry'd t'other day for fear my brother shou'd be angry with him for it'. And later, in June of the same year, she wrote, 'There is a vast friendship between William and Miss Conway; they play all day at being the Duke and Duchess of Richmond, and kissing eternally as they do'. Anne Conway – afterwards Mrs Damer – and the Duchess of Richmond were half-sisters. From Holland House the same month she wrote, 'William lives with the haymakers and the sheep shearers'.

The Kildares arranged for their two elder boys to go to Eton the following year, 1758. Their cousins, Stephen – known in the family as 'Ste' – and Charles Fox were already there. Lady Caroline Fox, who was making all the arrangements, wrote to her sister in July, 1758, to say that the boys would board at Mrs Milward's house. 'Mrs Milward will be in a better house by the time your boys come, I should say in a better situation, for as to the house she now goes to she must build to it; and the present way of settling is that Ste and William are to lie together. Ophaly a bed to himself in the same room, and Charles in a little one by them, for neither Ophaly or Charles like to have bedfellows; besides, they kick off the clothes so that the other boys don't like to lie with them, and I'm told Ste and Fitzy [William's nickname] agree mighty well; pray ask them if they approve. This is only for a time, because they will be quite accommodated by spring; your boys and Bolle will have a room to themselves and my boys and David ... Till her house is done, Mr Bolle and David are intended to lie at the house she now has, which is very near the other. The great hurry of her moving to a worse house is because that she now has is just out of bounds, which the masters object to'.

Mr Bolle was in charge of the FitzGeralds. He arranged for them to be placed under Mr Young, who was also the Foxes' tutor. On 12 September, 1758, William and his brother arrived at Eton. At that time Eton boys enjoyed much greater liberty than they do now. There was, however, a limit set to their independence. While William was there 40 or 50 boys, including himself and Charles Fox, revolted and went in a body to the Salt Hill Inn. The head master, Dr Barnard, having been informed by the landlord that the boys were in his house, directed him to allow them to remain as long as they had any money, but no longer. Having feasted for some days and spent all their money, the boys were obliged to return to the school, where they were flogged.

At Eton William FitzGerald and Charles Fox's names were carved together on a panel of the wall of the Upper School. And it was at Eton that the two began their lifelong friendship. Lord Kildare decided that his boys would spend only the long vacation in Ireland. The Christmas and Easter holidays they were to stay with the Foxes at Holland House. So it was not until April, 1759, when he crossed to England, that Lord Kildare saw his sons again. They had grown beyond recognition. Lord Kildare arrived in London on 18 April, and the boys were there to greet him. The following day he wrote to his wife that they had met him in the street, and that they were so much grown and looked so well, 'that when they came up to the chaise I did not recollect them at first. I don't think it is possible for them to be better, and I hear they are extremely good in every particular. Poor Ste looks very ill, and is full of motions. I think Mr Fox and Lady Caroline look extremely well'. Stephen, the Foxes' eldest son, who became second Lord Holland, was a delicate boy and suffered from St Vitus' Dance.

Lord Kildare stayed on in London after his sons returned to Eton, and on 12 May we find him writing to the Countess, '... I received a letter today from our little George, desiring a great many things as other boys have to wear at school. I return'd his letter, that Bolle might see what William and he wanted, and wrote to George that he might desire Bolle to get them'.

Lady Caroline Fox often visited the boys at Eton. On one occasion she took William for a long ride to the Duke of Cumberland's Park and Island. The boys 'delighted' in her visits. She wrote frequently to her sister to give her news of her children, and to tell her how their characters were developing. Towards the end of this same year William was already beginning to show that he had a will of his own, for on 29 November Lady Caroline wrote, 'I don't perceive any disagreements more than is usual among boys of the same age between your two. Fitzy is not very good-humoured certainly, but he goes his own way a good deal, and George loves him of all things. I do believe he loves Charles better, they are more suited. William don't at all enter into any of their amusements, and yet he is a mighty agreeable boy in his own way'. In April the following year (1760) she wrote, 'Your boys are charming well. But Lord Ophaly is, dear little soul, so very idle the masters say ... William says his brother's only ambition is to be a buck. William really improves and grows a charming boy'.

In 1761, on his father being created a Marquess, William became by courtesy 'Lord William FitzGerald'. In August he was ill and was attended by Dr Robert Adair, the surgeon, in whose opinion William should eat less and have a horse kept for him, since he did not care for cricket or other games.

At this time amateur theatricals were fashionable, and during the Easter holidays of 1762 the young cousins acted two plays at Holland House – *Creusa* and *Tom Thumb*. In the latter, a farce by Fielding, William took the part of the Princess Huncamunca, and according to his father, 'made a fine jolly, bold-looking girl'; while Lady Caroline Fox recorded that he did the part 'with humour and fun, then he look'd it to perfection, a fine overgrown handsome miss'.

Now that William was thirteen and growing up, Lord and Lady Kildare began to think of a profession for him. Perhaps his mother's mind went back to the time he was eight, when he 'lived with the hay-makers and sheep shearers'; for in December, 1762, she wrote to her husband from Castletown, where she was staying with her sister, Lady Louisa Conolly: 'If William has a turn for anything I think it is farming, but as you say he loves nothing with a degree of passion to excel in it; he is a fine boy too and far from silly.' Lady Caroline Fox, now Lady Holland, was also concerned for her nephew's happiness, but her ideas were moving in a different direction; a month or two earlier she had written to Lady Kildare, '... If Lord William is intended for the army I wonder you don't send him to some of the military academies which are the fashion here now, riding and fencing would I think make him more active *et le dégourdir un peu*'. And '... William has not parts for school learning, which makes it so unpleasant for him. I want you to enquire about the military academy; there is one by Holland House where Lord Howard, and Lady M Churchill's son is, both designed for the army'. Three years were now to pass before a final decision about William's profession was made; then, on 18 September, 1765, when he was sixteen years old, he received a commission, as cornet, in General Honeywood's troop of horse.

A week later, on 26 September, his elder brother, George, Earl of Ophaly, died after a long illness. William became Earl of Ophaly and his father's heir. New responsibilities had fallen on him. Lord Kildare decided that his son's education must be broadened. He would send him abroad; first to a military academy near Paris, and then to join the Hollands who were to make the Grand Tour of Europe. William would not only travel; he would stay long enough in certain cities to study the art of fortification and war.

On 25 April, 1766, Lady Holland wrote from Piccadilly to her sister, '... I hear William is coming soon to us. I shall be happy to see him, and rejoice to hear he is to be sent abroad, because I am convinced 'tis the least bad thing one can do with them at that age, notwithstanding the inconveniences that attend it'. And, five days later, '... I rather hope

Paris will not be the place fixed on for him; 'tis London removed only, for such heaps of English go every year there, that the young men scarcely ever see any French company, and the English one meets abroad are seldom what one would choose'. But Paris it was to be.

Came the third week in May, and Lady Holland was 'agreeably surprised dear sister, last Wednesday at coffee to see Lord Kildare and dear William walk in. The former I think looks as well as he did two years ago, and the latter much improved; if he held up his head he would be an exceeding fine figure'. A few days later she wrote, 'I like your William very much, dear sister, so does everybody; his manner is genteel, polite, and pleasing; he is exceeding handsome, but his person wants to be a little fashion'd, which a few months at an Academy will complete. I understand his father purposes sending him to one, and in the winter I hope he will meet us at Naples, where I believe it is almost determined for us to go; our young people will like it so much better, and my only objection was the terrible length of the journey, which all the women who have gone – and several have – tell me is paid by the beauty of it ... only think of crossing Alps and Appenines. If Lady Mary should not be breeding they go with us, so does Charles.' Lady Mary Fitzpatrick was the eldest daughter of the Earl of Upper Ossory; earlier this year she had married Stephen Fox. Lady Holland was undoubtedly very fond of William. In June she wrote, '... William will be very welcome, and make us happy in his company, wherever we are'.

William was in love, for the first time, with Lady Catherine Annesley; but amiable as always, he seems to have quite fallen in with his father's schemes. 'Poor William!' wrote Lady Holland, 'love at his age is very warm and very sincere generally. Who is Lady Catherine Annesley? Absence will I suppose cure him.' It did.

By the beginning of July William's arrangements for his departure were completed. The faithful Mr Bolle, his Swiss tutor, who had cared for him at Eton, was to travel with him. He was to be at the French Academy for three months; the Hollands would not be setting out on their travels until the end of September, and William would join them at Lyons, about a fortnight later. Meanwhile Lord and Lady Holland had gone to Kingsgate, their house by the sea in the Isle of Thanet. It was from here that Lady Holland wrote, on 4 July, 1766, 'I came yesterday to dinner, and last night dear William came by summer time; it was quite kind in him to come and take leave of Lord Holland. This morning at nine he set out for Dover. He has delightful weather and a fair wind. He seem'd sorry to leave England, but I hope the journey will prove both useful and agreeable to him'.

ACKNOWLEDEGEMENTS

I would like to thank the Trustees of the National Library of Ireland for kindly allowing me to quote extracts from the letters of William, 2nd Duke of Leinster, which I have edited with my husband for the Irish Manuscripts Commission.

I should like to acknowledge the assistance given me, amongst others, by Dr RI Best, and by Professor Sir Gavin de Beer, F.R.S., the authority on travel and travellers in the eighteenth century. I also desire to thank the Provost of Eton College for giving me permission to reproduce the portrait of Charles James Fox by Reynolds.

The chief books which I have consulted in the course of writing my book are given in the Bibliography; I found especially helpful Professor Mead's standard work on the Grand Tour in the eighteenth century.

1

PARIS – LYONS – MARSEILLES

Delightful weather and a fair wind: in these conditions the passage from Dover to Calais could be made in three hours. The packet boats, which sailed two or three times a week, were comfortable. The fare was half a guinea for a gentleman, and five shillings for a servant. For the journey from Calais to Paris a post chaise could be hired for the sum of two guineas and a half; it would follow the post route through Boulogne, Montreuil, Abbeville, Amiens, Chantilly and St Denis. At St Denis, the last town on the route, the traveller might see the Gothic abbey, with the black and white marble sepulchres of the royal house of France; the wax representations, made from death masks, of the later French kings; the Crown jewels of France, the golden and diamond crown of Charlemagne, worn by the French kings at their coronation, his sceptre, his sword, his spurs, and his ivory chessmen – each one as big as the fist of a man – Roland's horn and the sword of Joan of Arc – all of these treasures at the doorway to the capital.

William, Earl of Ophaly – as he then was – left England, accompanied by his Swiss tutor, Mr Bolle, on 4 July 1766. William's letters do not start until three months later, but it is not hard to imagine the excitement the seventeen-year-old Earl must have felt on landing for the first time on the European continent. He probably followed the conventional route to Paris and made straight for the academy near the capital, which was to be his home for the next three months. There he would learn riding and fencing and the science of fortification; for it was his father, the Marquess of Kildare's especial wish that he should make himself proficient in the military profession. He was inclined to be fat, and the exercise on horseback would help him to keep a good figure. A portrait of William as a young man, painted by Sir Joshua Reynolds, shows him as being good-looking, with well-defined features, a docile and gentle expression. He is dressed in a fur-edged, fur-lined red velvet coat, long silk waistcoat, silk knee-breeches and stockings. His white shirt has lace ruffles at the neck and cuffs.

Paris in the 1760s was beautiful. No doubt William's education included frequent visits to the city. Like Doctor Johnson, probably the first thing he did was to buy himself some French clothes – indeed, the amount of money the young man spent on his clothes while making his Grand Tour was prodigious; we get a picture of his tutor interminably putting out and folding away fabulous coats and waistcoats and breeches made of silks and satins embroidered with gold and silver. Along the wide boulevards, with their gravel walks, were large houses with balconies and open gardens with spreading trees giving plenty of shade; these belonged to the French nobility. The air was fresh and there was no black smoke. However hot the summer days might be, the large houses with their high rooms were kept cool and airy by leaving the immense windows and doors open, and by having jalousies to keep out the sun. The streets were filled with all kinds of carriages, dirty, shabby hackney coaches, black leather two-wheeled vehicles drawn by a man – and the numerous and splendid equipages of the nobles. The ladies drove about in glass and gilded berlins, wearing hoops and masses of curls, rouge and lace liveries. At home these fine ladies were forever at their needlework. The young men passed their time with the opera girls.

Such was life for the nobility and well-to-do. But for the poor, things were very different. The streets in which they lived were narrow, mean and dilapidated, and full of beggars. Here the tall houses contained a different family on every floor. The shops were unimpressive, particularly the butchers. Liver, lights and offal were cut out in slices and sold on small tables in almost every street and there were monstrous black sausages in great guts or bladders and boiled sheep's head. The dirty yellow Seine water, in which the washerwomen washed the linen of Paris, was unwholesome to drink and fresh water was on sale. The commonest wine was Burgundy; there was also Mousseux, a sparkling wine. At night the streets and quays were lighted with lanterns, placed wide apart, of a green glass in small panes set in lead. They were hung high across the streets in the middle by slender cords and gave little light. During full moon they were never lit. The passer-by was always liable to come upon unpleasant spectacles. Criminals were executed publicly; sometimes in the evening by torchlight, sometimes before the great door of Notre Dame. They were either hanged, or broken alive on the wheel. A man broken on the wheel could take eleven hours to die. And the death penalty was inflicted for so small an offence as breaking into a house and stealing two or three silver tumblers.

Such, then, in all its splendour and its misery, its glory and its squalor, was the Paris of his Majesty Louis XV, King of France.

Sightseeing must have occupied a good deal of William's time. There were the three great royal palaces to be visited – the Tuilleries, the Louvre, the Palais Royal inhabited by the Orleans family – which were full of pictures which had to be seen and admired. There were the lesser palaces – Sully, Richelieu, Mazarin – and those of the other great French families who prided themselves on their houses being worth a sightseeing visit; all of which contained statues and paintings of the first order. At the close of the day it was pleasant to walk in the Tuilleries gardens; the promenade was a great social custom, and the gardens of the palaces had been carefully laid out to provide walks. The Place de Louis XV, now Place de la Concorde, with its famous equestrian statue of the King, had recently been built. Especially popular was the promenade along the fortifications. Paris being walled in, the ramparts, more than half round the whole city, were adorned with four rows of trees, in the centre of which was a broad road for coaches, and on each side shady walks. Upon these ramparts were to be seen, every fine evening, many of the people of fashion taking the air in their coaches, which were attractively painted with a variety of pastoral scenes. There was the Bastille to be looked at, and the Invalides. The latter, designed for the same purpose as the Chelsea Hospital, contained about 3,000 maimed soldiers. No doubt visits to Versailles and Fontainebleau – to see the King of France – were included in William's itinerary. He may have visited St Germain, with its recollection of his great-great-grandfather's brother – James II. Then there were the operas and plays. The theatres began early; at the Comédie Française, which was in the Tuilleries, the show was over just after eight in the evening. In his spare time, William might drink coffee, tea or chocolate at a café. Or he could look in at the Cabinet Littéraire in the Rue Neuve des Petits Champs, and for four livres a month have the privilege of reading the English newspapers. Without doubt these three months spent by William at the academy near Paris must have been both profitable and pleasant.

Meanwhile, in England, William's aunt, Lady Holland, was preparing for *her* Grand Tour; when she would join her nephew at Lyons.

Although she had never made the Grand Tour, it was not her first visit abroad. She had been to France and the Netherlands as a child and again in 1763; and to France in 1765, when she had stayed in the great country houses. She liked the French turn of life and conversation. In her opinion, there was great truth in the French saying: '*les français sont heureux, les anglais cherchent à l'être*.'

She thought that every woman past 30 who understood the language, and who liked conversation better than cards, would prefer Paris to London. For herself she declared she preferred Kingsgate life to either.

As Lady Holland supervised the packing of the many clothes she would take with her, her thoughts were of the journey that lay ahead; of the long, straight roads – built by the *corvée* or forced labour system, itself a cause of the French Revolution – bordered by tall, straight trees, and running through flat hedgeless country; of the excessively dirty inns, 'bad beyond imagination' – the French people never stayed in them; when they travelled, which was seldom, it was the fashion to go day and night without stopping to sleep – and worst horror of all, the crossing over of the Alps and Appenines. Her anticipation turned to dread. But she comforted herself with the hope that the journey would benefit Lord Holland, who was in poor health, and who was to make his way from Marseilles to Naples by sea. So, with Mrs Fannen, the steward's wife, to help her, her mind left the long straight roads, the dirty inns, and the sound of galloping French hooves stopping neither by night nor by day, and concentrated upon whether she should take with her this dress or that, this green cloak or the blue one lying over there on the bed.

When all the packing was done, Lady Holland went to her closet and sat down at her table to write to her beloved sister, Lady Kildare – William's mother – in Ireland. She was at Kingsgate, her house by the sea in the Isle of Thanet. 'This is probably the last letter I shall write this side of the water; Tuesday next week we embark from this door. The weather at present is heavenly. I hope you enjoy it. I can enjoy nothing with the thoughts of crossing this odious sea.'

On her previous visit to France, in 1763, she had likewise departed from her own door; although with a very fair wind the passage took four hours instead of the three from Dover, she considered the comfort of waiting for a fair wind in her own house rather than in a bad inn worth an hour more at sea.

She had appointed William to be with her party at Lyons on 8

October, as it was thought better to cross the Alps before the rainy season came on. Her son Charles left her on 20 September; he was to join William in Paris on his way to Lyons. Lady Holland, on the other hand, was to avoid the capital, and to go through Champagne and Burgundy. Once more she bid her sister adieu; 'you comprehend the fidget and feel I have I'm sure. What a great part of one's life is passed in preparation for the future and how little the present is enjoy'd in quiet.'

On 23 September, Lord and Lady Holland and their party crossed the 'odious sea', and drove, along wide roads planted with willows, poplars and elms, by way of St Omer – 'a fine town, full of Irish Papists' – to Arras. Here they had to wait for horses in a nasty inn. Lord Holland, however, was bearing the journey well. Lady Holland was enjoying herself. The road was new to her, and she admired both the countryside and the towns with their fortifications. The weather was perfect. She was in excellent spirits. And she was looking forward to seeing William at Lyons.

The drive from Arras to Lyons was tedious and long. Otherwise it was pleasant: weather, roads – everything was in their favour. Lord Holland had at times been fatigued, but in the main had borne the journey surprisingly well. He had even put on a little weight. From Arras they drove through Picardy into Champagne. Half a day was spent at Rheims. 'There is in it,' observed Lady Holland, 'the finest old Gothic Church I ever saw.' The country around was open and ugly, like Wiltshire. Further south in the same province the road was very beautiful from a view of the river Marne in the valley, and high hills covered with vines, parks and woods – a very romantic pretty prospect all the way. But when they came into Burgundy, Lady Holland found that the cheerfulness, gaiety, richness and beauty of the country was not to be described. Dijon, the capital, was a most agreeable town, and the road from there to Lyons, all through the same province, was 'really heavenly'; the feel of the air was so pure, soft and charming. 'The river Saône which runs thro' it, and meets the Rhône here, is as fine as the Thames; the valley thro' which it runs full of meadows, corn, flax, and every kind of culture.' The hills on each side, covered with wood, vines, villages, hamlets, gentlemen's houses, churches, made altogether the most delightful scene. 'Without exaggeration you drive miles together with a view of much prospect – only far exceeding it – as you see from Richmond Hill'.

It was the time of the *vendange* – the grapepicking season. The vineyards being in some places close to the road, they stopped the carriage, and for sixpence ate as many delicious grapes as they pleased. Lady Holland found the country vastly peopled, and the peasants looking more prosperous than those she had seen elsewhere in France. The peasant women's dress struck her as being comical and pretty. At one town the 'common people' had what they called *couvre-chefs*, a square muslin handkerchief pinned like a veil on their heads; it looked neat and pretty. Those in the fields wore a little black high-crowned hat. She thought it both neat and decent that the 'common people' should have a particular dress, and not as it was in England, all alike. However, she did recall that once at Margate a girl who had come to sell eggs and cucumbers was dressed in a blonde fly cap, as they called it, and silk gown.

They arrived at Lyons on 5 October, and expected William Ophaly and Charles Fox to arrive from Paris during the next day or two. They were to remain at Lyons for a week to prepare for their journey over the Alps.

Lady Holland, like nearly every other member of the aristocracy of her time, recognised two kinds of person in the world: the people and – the *common* people. It is impossible to see Europe through the aristocratic Grand Tourist's eyes unless we try also to understand the mentality of the time. And this mentality was largely formed by tradition, which in its turn had produced the social conditions of the time. The French Revolution had not happened – that is the most important thing to remember. The state of affairs was not so bad in England – they had had their revolutions and partly learnt their lessons. But on the continent of Europe the feudal system lingered on. Abuses, unjust privileges and slavery were still rampant. Any good practices the system may ever have had were long since dead and gone. European political theorists and philosophers – and a tiny handful of English travellers such as Chesterfield and, later, Arthur Young – saw the rot and wrote about it. The average tourist did not. Beauty there certainly was: in architecture, sculpture, painting, dress and music. But it was the beauty of the orchid growing in a cesspool. European life in the 1760s went on much as it had done for hundreds and hundreds of years. Twenty years or so later came the grand upheaval. The mind of Europe awoke and was changed. And was to impress itself gradually upon the whole world.

The development of history had produced variations in the

system from one country to another. Let us look a little closer at the conditions prevailing in those parts of Europe in which Lord Kildare travelled and lived during the three years of his study abroad. Take France, for instance, theoretically the power of the French King was absolute. But no monarch, however benevolent, could have pushed through the necessary reforms against the will of the nobles and Catholic hierarchy; nor could he have hoped to unravel the tangle into which the finances of the country had fallen. Local governments were interfered with by the central authority; rules and regulations were constantly altered; administrative confusion reigned. The nobles and clergy were the privileged classes. Numbering but a thirtieth part of the twenty-six millions in France, they enjoyed an enormous proportion of the nation's income; and, if we exclude the public domain from the estimate, they owned one-half of all the land in France. They were almost entirely exempt from taxation. The full burden of taxation, fell, therefore, on the third estate, which comprised the rest of the population – the peasants, working-classes in the towns, small tradesmen, merchants, bankers, men of letters, members of the learned professions, and so on. The nobles had deserted their estates in the time of Louis XIV – at the request of the monarch – and lived at Versailles or Paris. They continued to draw money from their estates, and their younger brothers continued to be appointed to rich and advantageous positions within the church. In addition to being exempt from taxation, they were also free from public burdens. No *corvée* system for them; no compulsory military service, no quartering of soldiers upon them. They had many privileges surviving from feudalism – all detrimental to the peasant. One such privilege was the right to sell their wine in the market 30 or 40 days before the peasant, another to claim a certain proportion of the peasant's fruit or wine or grain etc – privileges that seemed increasingly irrational, since what had caused them to come into being no longer existed; privileges that were an invitation to revolution. The French noble class was, therefore, in strong contrast to the English aristocracy – a sturdy support of the social order and the constitution. The princes of the church levied their own taxes or tithes on the peasants and the rest of the third estate, and received a vast annual income from voluntary offerings and bequests. The minor clergy were neglected and underpaid and were very often little better off than the starving peasants whom they served. The peasants were indeed hard-pressed under the burdens – financial and otherwise – imposed upon them by government, nobles and church. Exhausted by excessive toil and kept poor by oppressive taxation, they could never hope to rise. Consequently, although many of the towns were relatively prosperous, the small villages and rural hamlets were often just wretched collections of filthy hovels occupied by half-starved peasants.

Charles James Fox was the same age as Ophaly. Together they had been at Eton; and now together they were to make the Grand Tour. There is a portrait, painted by Sir Joshua Reynolds in 1765, of the young Charles Fox, which he gave to Dr Barnard, the head master of Eton as a leaving present, now in the Provost's Lodge at Eton. It shows a dark young man with bushy eyebrows, wearing a mulberry coat and waistcoat; the face is pale, and turned slightly to one side; the expression is simple and direct, and the young man seems about to turn towards the artist and say something. This picture personifies energy in repose. For a portrait without hands Reynolds charged only twenty-five guineas; this must, therefore, have been the price of Fox's picture, for the hands do not show. These portraits were a substitute for the tip which the young gentlemen were required until 1868 to give to their head master, with infinite discretion, when they left the school; Dr Barnard, head master from 1754 to 1765, first had the idea of asking his more interesting pupils – brains as well as birth were what appealed to him – to give him portraits of themselves instead of money.

So the young Fox, already a man of the world who had travelled abroad and acquired a taste for drinking and gambling – thanks to his father's habit of supplying him, when only in his fifteenth year, with a certain number of guineas every night for the purpose of speculating at the gaming table – arrived in Paris to seek out his cousin. His intention was no doubt to rush him round the pleasures of Paris before setting out with him on the road to Lyons.

Now the great day came. William's dearest wish was about to be fulfilled. For weeks and months he had been looking forward to this journey; overland to Marseilles, the long sea journey to Naples. We can picture the two young cousins – well wrapped up, for it was October – leaving their Paris lodging early in the morning, accompanied by William's tutor, Mr Bolle, and jumping into the post chaise. How they must have talked and talked! We can imagine them bubbling over with delighted chatter. Charles Fox, we know, was an extremely fast talker. No doubt Mr Bolle pointed out objects of interest to them on the way; for, as tutor, it was his job to see that William got the maximum amount of educational benefit from his travels.

In the days of walled towns there was usually a swift transition from city to open country; and such was the case at Paris. Less than a hundred yards beyond the city walls were flocks of sheep peacefully grazing by the roadside. The little horses that drew the chaise went three abreast, one of them ridden by the postillion. Outside the carriage sat the private servant; or he might ride on horseback. There was, too, the courier who rode ahead to order fresh horses at the next posting-house.

The chaise horses were unable to travel fast owing to the hard surface of the roads. Many of the main roads were good and clean, paved with stone. 'Of all modern nations,' wrote Voltaire, 'France and the little country of the Belgians are the only ones that have roads worthy of antiquity.' Off the beaten track, however, and through mountainous country, the roads were generally less good; sometimes, indeed, they were terrible.

The journey from Paris to Lyons took about five days. When he stopped for the night at an inn, Willliam must frequently have passed through a crowd of beggars that would often collect round the door of the inn on the arrival of wealthy-looking foreigners. William and Charles held similar political views throughout their lives. Is it probable that what they saw together while travelling abroad – the extreme poverty and wretchedness of the 'common people' – helped to form their later judgements on political and social matters, and gave Charles his understanding and approval of the principles, though not, of course, the excesses, of the French Revolution?

William would probably have shared his aunt's opinion about the inns: that they were bad 'beyond imagining'. But if the beds were dirty and damp and the sanitation non-existent or primitive, the food on the whole was good: even in those days French cooking was celebrated. For their personal safety Charles and William had little need to fear: highway robbery had been almost stamped out.

There were three different routes to Lyons: two post-roads and a third used by the diligence. The post-roads diverged after passing through the forest of Fontainebleau. Which of these two roads the cousins took is not recorded. But we may reasonably conclude that they took the one which was by far the more picturesque. This followed the valley of the river Yonne, and crossed rich country full of vineyards and orchards, villages and walled towns, chateaux and

9

flocks of sheep, and here and there a peasant ploughing with a don-key, a thin cow, and a billy-goat, yoked together. Between Auxerre and Dijon, a distance of 32 leagues, the road led over the wild moun-tains of the Cote d'Or with their wolf-infested forests. Jolting along the rough mountain road, the carriage descended into Dijon, from where the route would have been the same as that taken by Lady Holland a day or two earlier.

'Lord Ophaly is arrived with Charles from Paris, looking very well, and is grown genteel,' wrote Lady Holland from Lyons on 6 October to Lady Kildare; 'he will write himself to you. He has seen more French than you imagine at the camp; he lived chiefly with them.' When we recall that William would have had to buy himself new French clothes at his first arrival in the capital, and that he had spent three months in French company, it is hardly surprising to find that he had acquired polished manners along with his Gallic dress.

What would have been William's first impressions of Lyons? Great wealth side by side with great poverty; jostling crowds hustling through narrow, dirty, badly-paved streets; houses with ragged paper windows; palaces where great merchants lived magnificently; inns cel-ebrated for their splendid show of plate and their excellent food; small squares; houses and churches and commercial buildings huddled closely together on the long, narrow peninsula formed by the waters of the great rivers Rhône and Saône – indeed, the chief impression of this city was one of water. The city was still largely medieval, although some rebuilding had taken place. But plans were already in hand for the reclamation of the marshy tip of the peninsula by the sculptor, Antoine-Michel Perrache.

Since William was to see so much that was Roman, it was fitting that he should start his Grand Tour with the ancient Lugdunum, which became the capital of Celtic Gaul. No doubt his tutor had taught him something of its history. It must have been with interest and not a little pride that he learned that a great part of its prosperi-ty was due to the Florentine bankers who had settled there in 1450; for had not his own family, the Geraldines, sprung from the famous Gherardini of Florence? And with his love of fine clothes he would have been equally interested in the other great industry upon which Lyons had built up her prosperity and which by now had become the primary source of the city's wealth – the silk trade. His young imag-ination would have been fired with the story of its origins: how two

Persian monks were sent by Justinian to China and returned to Constantinople about AD 550 with a bamboo rod in which they had a stock of silk-worm eggs; and of how from the silk worms reared from this consignment all the silk-rearing countries of the west were stocked. Fresh from his military academy, William was no doubt eager to learn about the city's origin as a Roman fort; its sack five centuries later – its ruins, like so many Roman ruins, long afterwards being quarried for building stones; its subsequent growth on the peninsula, protected between two rivers, when it could be surrounded by water by cutting a ditch at the foot of the hill of Croix-Rousse. Indeed, Lyons had ever been a vital point in the defence of France.

William was welcomed into the intimate circle of the Holland family. We have already seen how close he was to his aunt. He was no less attached to his uncle. Hated by a fleeced English public, Lord Holland was adored by his family. 'As will always be the case with a man of strong intelligence and commanding powers, who has the gift of forgetting himself in others, there was no limit to the attachment which he inspired, and the happiness which he spread around him.'[*] His devoted wife, his precocious children, upon all of whom he lavished an unbounded affection, shared with him similar tastes and pursuits; appreciated him as he did them, having, however, too much sense and individuality to allow their estimation of one another to sink to the level of mutual flattery. Leaving behind him the cares of office and the unfaithfulness of his friends, and surrounded by his family, Lord Holland could enjoy domestic happiness and hope for better health.

In addition to William, Charles, and Lord and Lady Holland, the party now consisted of Stephen Fox and his wife, Lady Mary, both of whom had just arrived at Lyons, Harry Fox, the Hollands' youngest son, now aged eleven, Clotworthy Upton, afterwards Lord Templeton, and Mr Bolle.

Stephen Fox had married the previous April, at Holland House, Lady Mary Fitzpatrick, daughter of Lord Ossory and a relation of the Duke of Bedford. Ste – as his family called him – was good-natured, and enormously fat. Lord Carlisle, a friend of the family, and about Charles' age, considered there was 'something so laughable in Stephen's character and conduct that, though he were broke upon the wheel, or torn between four wild horses like Damien, the persons

* Sir G. Otto Trevelyan: *The Early History of Charles James Fox.*

who live the most with him would never be grave or serious upon any calamity happening to him'. He entered Parliament at the same time as his younger brother, but his political gifts were greatly inferior, and he did not succeed. Taking little part himself in public affairs, his anxiety about them amused his friends. He would write to the newspapers and sign himself 'a stander-by who has fears'. Like his brother he became a heavy gambler; in one evening he lost thirteen thousand pounds. His great size never seemed to worry him. On the occasion of the bringing in of a bill to abolish the observance of the thirtieth of January, he amused the House of Commons by suggesting that it was unfair to force everyone to be abstemious, when the martyred King's descendants – meaning himself and his brother Charles, who by then was also very fat – so obviously never fasted. On another occasion, at a fancy dress ball, a Smithfield butcher pursued him, digging him in the ribs and trying to guess his weight; until two exceedingly merry Wives of Windsor, calling him their Falstaff, took him off with them for the remainder of the evening.

What of Lady Mary? For Stephen Fox, Lady Mary Fitzpatrick was the perfect wife. She did not mind his huge figure nor his other shortcomings; quite simply, she loved him. And she gave him a son who long outlived both his parents and became distinguished as the third Lord Holland. Her mother-in-law had the highest opinion of her. 'The more I think of it,' she wrote, 'the more I think how lucky Ste is to have got such a girl among the present misses.' Lady Holland called her 'my pretty Mary'; Lady Sarah Bunbury, 'a little blessed angel'.

It will be recalled that the party was to remain at Lyons for a week in order to prepare for their journey over the Alps. In fact they were detained longer on account of some springs being put on the carriage for the Italian journey. The family was to divide, Lady Holland going with Ste, Lady Mary, Harry and Mr Upton overland, while Lord Holland was to take William and Charles down the Rhône to Marseilles, thence by sea to Naples.

Shortly after his arrival at Lyons, William wrote to his mother:

LYONS, October 16th, 1766. My dearest Mother, I hope you received my letter dated the 9th of this month. I believe we leave this place on Sunday next. Lady Holland proceeds by land for Naples. We go from this to Avignon by water; we shall be two days. If the weather is fine it'll be very pleasant; if it is bad it will be very disagreeable as it is a very bad contrived boat. I am glad that Lord Holland means to sleep ashore; for, as he first intended, to sleep in the boat wou'd have been very bad. He, thank God, continues well and in good spirits. I think rather mends every day. I hope the sea air that he is so fond of won't be too much, as we shall be a good while at sea.

William was greatly looking forward to the Italian part of his tour. So in his letter to his mother he continued:

I propose myself great pleasure in Italy, as it is a country I have long wished to see. I hear there is good riding and fencing at Naples – two very good and very agreeable exercises. The worst is the bad Italian. There is to be great doings this year. The King of Naples comes of age and is to be married and crowned.

William went on to describe how he was spending his time at Lyons:

I was yesterday to see a convent of monks called the Chartreuse.* They are a set of very religious monks that never speak to one another but Monday and Thursday. They have each of them a cell, which contains two rooms and a little garden for them to work in. They all dine together of a Sunday and must not speak. They never eat meat or broth made of meat; they eat nothing but fish and eggs, and that is given them through a little door made in the wall.

This is a great silk manufacturing town; remarkable for brocaded silks. It is very pretty to see them make them.

How William and Charles must have delighted in the taffetas, velvets, brocades, ribbons, satins, and cloth of gold and silver. William could hardly have enjoyed more the necessity imposed upon every young nobleman travelling abroad of buying expensive and magnificent clothes; and Charles, when he wore his odd little French hat and his red heels and later when he dashed from Paris to Lyons in order to choose patterns for his embroidered waistcoats, was anticipating the time when he would be the leader of London fashion.

The deliciousness of the autumn in the Rhône valley did not pass William by unnoticed. He could not help comparing it favourably with the damp climate of his Irish home:

* This monastery is not, of course, to be confused with the Grand Chartreuse, which is near Grenoble.

I suppose all except you are warming themselves over the fire. Today is the coldest day I have felt since I came to France, yet I am sitting close to the window with it open. I suppose you are still and likely to remain at Carton, which will soon begin to look dismal by the fall of the leaves.

But it was, after all, October. And three days later William was writing:

The weather here is grown cold; the morning and evening are very cold.

Social activities were not neglected:

We yesterday went to see a country house of Madame la Comtesse de Varras. It is about a mile out of town. It stands very high; it commands the finest prospect in the world. The ground rises and falls prettily. A fine view of the Saône; a great deal of wood. The view is directly like the views about Bath, only in large.

Lady Holland, too, was impressed with the delightful view from the house, from which could be seen the rivers Saône and Rhône winding in a rich cultivated valley, the town of Lyons, and the hills rising on the other side covered with houses and vineyards. The house stood on a hill, to the south of which was a fine long natural *terrasse;* behind the house and *terrasse*, to the north, was an oak wood on rising ground. 'It was,' wrote Lady Holland, 'one of those fine October days described by Mme de Sévigné, *ces beaux jours de crystal d'octobre.*' There was orange trees and greenhouse plants out of doors. In the house itself, they learned, Henri IV had stayed. It had a large gallery 170 feet long with a large *salle de compagnie* adjoining it above stairs for the summer apartment; the autumn apartment below stairs, opening to a little garden full south, overlooking the view.

The rest of the time they spent in a variety of ways. One day they went to see the old Roman walls and baths – a first taste of the rich treasures of antiquity in store for them. Another day they went to a peasants' *fête* about a league from the town, where there was dancing, eating and junketing in the open air, which was 'vastly pretty'. They passed part of their time with Lady Mary Churchill, a natural daughter of Sir Robert Walpole, and her husband, Colonel Charles Churchill, natural son of General Churchill – nephew of the great Duke of Marlborough – by the celebrated actress, Mrs Oldfield. The Churchills, who had a house at Nancy, were in Lyons for a few days.

It was Lady Holland's belief that they travelled only from restlessness. Then there was the theatre – 'a very pretty one, the actors tolerable' – where they saw *La Chasse d'Henri Quatre*, a play based on Dodsley's *The King and the Miller of Mansfield.* Every morning William went to the riding school; he went for long walks, too, as he was anxious not to get fat. 'I wish my Ste,' lamented Lady Holland, 'would take the same method, but 'tis too late with him I fear now, his size is so enormous.'

By now Lady Holland was impatient to get over the Alps while the dry clear weather lasted; for she had heard that the journey being pleasant or otherwise depended entirely on the weather. Lord Holland had calculated her journey by the Italian post book; by stopping two days at Turin, three at Florence, and seven at Rome, she might, without travelling long journeys, be at Naples by 21 November. It will be recalled that they were delayed at Lyons owing to new springs being put on the carriage; this work was now nearly completed, and in a few days they would set out. Ste and Lady Mary Fox had already left for Geneva, where they were to see some old acquaintances of Ste, who under the famous Dr Tronchin had spent some time there a few years previously;[*] they were due to rejoin Lady Holland and her party at Turin.

On 19 October, William wrote:

> We leave this place Tuesday next. To be sure I rather should have liked to be of the land party; but I am very well content. As it is, as I am resolved not to be sick, and as it is in a large ship I dare say I shall keep my resolution. Lord Holland, Charles and I go down the fine river Rhône, which I am told is very pleasant. We shall be two days going to Avignon; from Avignon to Nîmes; from Nîmes to Arles; from do: to Aix in Provence and Marseilles, where I shall have the pleasure of writing to you again. Please God when I return from Italy, it will be over the Alps. I hope Lord Kildare will have no objection, if Ste Fox or any party should go to Venice to see the Carnival, to my going. Lord Holland, thank God, continues mending ... Bolle hopes you'll excuse his not writing this day as he has just been blooded of a little feverish cold, but I hope it'll be nothing at all. I hope that the fine climate of Naples will agree with him.

The week that they had intended spending in Lyons to prepare for

* During his stay in Geneva, Ste had become a friend of Voltaire, frequently visiting him at 'Les Délices'. Many years earlier, Henry Fox, too, had met Voltaire.

their journey over the Alps had grown to over a fortnight, owing to their 'nasty carriage' not being ready before. Then Lady Holland, Harry Fox and Clotworthy Upton set out on the road over the Alps to Turin; William, Lord Holland, Charles Fox and Mr Bolle boarded the river boat for Avignon.

William was unlucky to be going on a 'very bad contrived boat'; for some of them were very comfortable, having decks high enough to walk under. However, the journey was pleasant enough. Floating with the current, the boat passed between two ranges of mountains. On either side the grapes were being gathered in the autumn sun; little churches perched on top of many of the hills. The nights were passed in some of the numerous villages that lined the shores. At the bridge of St Esprit William and Charles disembarked. This bridge, built in a curve across the river, was the scene of many accidents, boats being sometimes wrecked on the piers while trying to shoot the arches. Coming upstream the boats were drawn by oxen, which swam through the arches, the driver sitting between the horns of the animal.

When he finally reached Marseilles, William wrote to his mother describing the journey:

MARSEILLES, the 29th October, 1766.
My dearest Mother ... Lord Holland, Charles and I arrived here on Tuesday last. We came down the Rhône. Lord Holland went as far as Avignon; Charles and I came no further than a place called Pont du St Esprit. From thence we went to Nîmes which is a city in Languedoc. It was a very great city in the time of the Romans. It is remarkable for the well preserved antiquities; there is a building that is called la Maison Quarrée, built thirty years before the birth of Christ. It is so well preserved that you hardly take it to be more than fifty years old; the columns are of the Corinthian order.

Nîmes was originally a Roman colony – Nemausus – settled by Augustus Caesar, after the battle of Actium. The Maison Carée, was the exquisite temple built in the style of the Parthenon in honour of Gaius and Lucius Caesar, the grandchildren of Augustus, by his daughter Julia, the wife of Agrippa.

In spite of the veneration in which this building was held, restoration was not always carried out with satisfactory results. On one occasion a small roof repair called forth from an Italian painter the angry exclamation, 'Zounds! what do I see? Harlequin's hat on the head of Augustus!' Arthur Young described it as 'beyond comparison the most light, elegant, and pleasing building' he had ever seen. Until 1789 it was used as a church. William goes on to describe the magnificent Roman amphitheatre, towards the erection of which Antonius Pius is said to have contributed a large sum of money, his family having originally belonged to Nîmes:

> There is also an amphitheatre built a hundred years later; it is reckoned the most complete of any that is remaining. It is oval; it is French measure 180 toise or English fathom in circumference the great diameter is 63, the small is 47, and the height is 10 toise 4 feet 6 inches. It is said to have contained 20 thousand people; and the foolish people have built all the inside with little dirty cabins.

At this point one is tempted to ask whether William got his figures from the local guide, or whether he had followed the advice contained in Nugent's guide-book, *Grand Tour* – the Baedeker of the period: "Tis proper also to be provided with maps, measures, prospective glasses, a mariner's compass and quadrant, and to be able to take the dimensions of things.' Nugent confirms that the amphitheatre was filled up with little houses of tradesmen; and he says that outside were squalid tenements. Only after the Revolution was its restoration undertaken. William and his friend then went to see the splendid Roman aqueduct built by Agrippa, that spans the Gard:

> There is also about twelve miles from the town a bridge called the Pont du Gard, it is said was built for the conveyance of water to the amphitheatre. It is in a bottom between two mountains. It has three bridges one a top the other. The height is twenty five fathoms 5 feet. The lower arches are six in number, 10 ditto 4 feet in height, in second row there is twelve arches, of 10 fathom 2 feet in height; the third row has 36 arches, 3 fathom 4 foot in height; and at the top there is a little cove passage where that water used to pass from one mountain to the other. They say it was built at the same time as the amphitheatre.
>
> We also saw what they call the Roman baths, which is but lately found out. They always knew there was a spring, which caused a little rivulet strong enough to turn a mill; and digging to find where the spring was they found underground remains of old bath, supposed to be made by the Romans. They have built little walls round them and have made a public parterre for everybody to walk.

Nîmes was considered by travellers a second Rome. The natives, who had organised a flourishing tourist business, took full advantage of gullible travellers; and were duly complained of by Smollett; William, however, had evidently been long enough in France to be immune from the attacks of these 'antiquarians' who peddled so-called Roman antiques, for he nowhere mentions them. In Charles he had the ideal companion. The boy who had caught his mother out on a point of Roman history before he was seven was by now a classical scholar. And he delighted in mathematics. These two seventeen-year-old boys found great pleasure in each other's company; and enormous stimulation from their first real contact with Roman civilisation.

Now they pushed on through Languedoc and Provence, the country of olive and fig trees, of vines and corn, on towards the sea coast. Marseilles was already a prosperous commercial city. Its harbour was crowded with the masts of many ships. Its quays were thronged with people from different nations. On the quays, too, the galley slaves were allowed to have little booths, at which they sat and worked, with one foot chained.

But the city had little of interest to detain the party. They were anxious to be off. Ships in the Mediterranean were still sometimes captured by Barbary pirates. And in spite of the enjoyment Lord Holland might get from the sea air of which he was so fond, it would be a relief to reach the harbour of Naples in safety. What there was to see at Marseilles they soon saw; and William concluded his letter thus:

> I believe we sail tomorrow. I dread the sea very much, for I went out a little way to sea today to see our ship and was very sick. But I hope after the first day it'll go off. This is a handsome town, well built, a fine quay and harbour for ships. The King of France's galleys are [here]; it is very shocking to see the poor people working with a great heavy chain to their legs.

2

NAPLES

However much William may have envied Lady Holland going over the Alps, he can hardly have counted himself the loser when he approached the Italian coast and the magnificent panorama of the Bay of Naples unfolded. His first sight of this wonderful place, dominated by the Castel Sant' Elmo and Vesuvius, with the further arm of the bay stretching out towards the distant hump of Capri, must have created a very deep impression. The sun-scorched houses climbed one above the other up the hill; centuries of building had gone into the making of the city. The last few years had seen an effervescence of building following upon King Charles' own example, and as a result of his policy of encouraging nobles to live in the capital in order to undermine their authority. Palaces, churches, triumphal arches had sprung up; and in many cases the designs had been carried out by such first rate architects as Vanvitelli and Ferdinando Sanfelice. Jumbled up among these architectural masterpieces were the squalid apartment houses of the extreme poor. The streets were so narrow as to be often mere passages. And the noise – from before dawn until after sunset the braying of asses, the hawkers' shouts, the rattling of cartwheels, the bleating of goats, and the incessant cries and jabber of its 300,000 inhabitants and its 40,000 half-naked *lazzaroni* who lived in the streets, made Naples the noisiest and liveliest city in all Italy. The women had beautiful hair in great quantity, which was seen to full perfection, their great occupation being to delouse one another in the street all day long in the sun.

On 11 November, after a very pleasant passage of eleven days, with fine weather all the way, William and his party disembarked, made their way along the quay, through the shouting crowds of seamen, citizens and beggars, and were soon comfortably installed in one of the best houses. Mr Bolle unpacked William's many fine clothes and put them all carefully away. William himself sat down by the open window and dashed off a line to his mother to let her know he had arrived safely. A week later, in a less hurried mood, he wrote again – this time a long letter full of all the things he had packed into those seven exciting days:

> NAPLES, November 17th, 1766. My dearest Mother, I hope you received my last letter of 11th inst., and that you are so kind as to forgive the shortness of it, as I was but just landed and the post going out, as it only goes out once a week ... We have a very good house, but the misfortune is that the best apartment is up three pairs of stairs, which is very disagreeable. Lord Holland is carried up and down. But it is the case with all the best houses of this town.
>
> We have the sea close to our windows. We have a side view of Vesuvius, but the burning is on the other side of us, so we see nothing but smoke in the day time, at night a redness in the sky. Charles Fox and I were there the other evening, but we did not go quite to the top, but just to see the lava, which runs down in streams; but it is nothing to what it was in April last, when it was in one stream of two miles broad and four long. It has been running ever since Good Friday last. The knowing ones seem to think it must stop soon, though the inhabitants about wish it to continue.
>
> Mr Hamilton, who is our Minister, is a great connoisseur; he is a very civil and obliging man, and so is his wife. They have been so obliging as to introduce Charles and I to almost all the first people here, who are very fond of the English.

Hamilton, who later became Sir William Hamilton, had arrived in Naples as British Envoy two years earlier. Once a week he and his first wife (a Miss Barlow, not the famous Emma Hart whom he married later) gave an evening party. Here his English guests met members of the great Neapolitan families, diplomats, cardinals. There was music, cards and billiards. But Hamilton is remembered today rather as an archaeologist than as a diplomat, his collection of Greek vases was subsequently purchased by the British Museum and it formed the groundwork for the present department of Greek and Roman antiquities.

Being of noble birth William had the entrée to all the ruling houses of Italy. At Naples there was more entertaining than in any other part of the peninsula. Following upon King Charles' revival of building, the nobles had erected themselves beautiful town palaces, many of which were enriched with Sanfelice's splendid and unusual double staircases. Up and down these fine stairs, preceded by pages carrying torches, passed and repassed the princes and princesses in their blue and gold, green and scarlet silks and satins, brocades and damasks. From the courtyard below came the sound of horses' hooves stamping and wheels crunching as the carriages rolled in and rolled away in a never-ending flow, until with the morning they returned to take the happy, dizzy, weary princes and princesses home to bed.

Most lavish of these hosts was the Prince of Francavilla. He and the Princess gave a dinner every night, to which distinguished English visitors were always invited.* They never sat down less than twelve people – sometimes as many as 40. Guests would arrive about nine o'clock, sup and play cards, and go home early. William enjoyed these evening parties, at which he was often present, more than any others to which he was invited. The Princess Marsico, for example, who also had a nightly assembly kept much later hours and had a great deal of cards, neither of which William cared for. Apart from the Francavillas, none of the nobility gave dinners at their assemblies. They found they could not afford to do so and at the same time keep up an appearance of great splendour. They preferred to live on a little macaroni and vegetables, and spend their money on equipages and servants.

We have been to two balls and concerts. One was at the Princess Francavilla. They danced English country dances, which the people of this country are very fond of; I am but a bad hand, and know no country dance. The other ball was at the Princess Bella Monte – one of the handsomest Neapolitan ladies. I am to go tonight after the opera to the Venetian Ambassador. In short, if Naples continues as agreeable as it is at present, it will be very pleasant; but what I hear it is not always so. But all these balls and concerts are for the Prince of Brunswick, who is here at present but goes on Wednesday. It is amazing the fatigue he undergoes here. He is up every morning at 6 o'clock and out seeing the curiosities all morning; he comes home about twelve, dresses himself and goes to a great dinner; afterwards to a ball, where he dances till two or three o'clock in the morning. He is very much liked here, he is so very civil to everybody. He dances out of mere complaisance, as the balls are made on purpose for him, and if he did not dance there would be no dancing ...

* Prince Charles of Meckenburg, brother of Queen Charlotte of England, was in Naples at this time – William writes, 'he is very good humoured, talks English very well'.

William was lucky to be in Naples at this time when so much entertaining was going on for the German prince. Karl Wilhelm
Ferdinand, an extremely popular young man of 31, was Hereditary
Prince of Brunswick; he succeeded his father as Duke in 1780. An
excellent soldier, he commanded the Austrian and Prussian armies at
the time of the French Revolution. His wife was Augusta, sister of
George III.

> I forgot to mention that I supped at the Princess Francavilla. Everything
> was very magnificent. But one course, and dessert, served very well and
> clean; silver plates, dishes, all very clean – which I never saw in France
> – and change knives and forks. I can't say it is the custom of the rest of
> the *noblesse*, as that is the *Northumberland House of the town*. The peo-
> ple here are very proud of their *noblesse*. I can't say much for the beau-
> ties of this town, as I think except five or six that are tolerably pretty the
> rest are hideous. None of them six to be compared to Lady Catherine
> Annesley or a great many other English or Irish. They are very ungen-
> teel in their manners, just like girls at a country assembly; if anything
> more vulgar, sitting with their handkerchiefs before them. They are
> very badly educated. I have not seen one that could make a curtsey or
> dance a minuet with the least grace. I saw last night a French lady, that
> is married to a Neapolitan, dance; it is not to be told the difference in
> her manner and the rest.
>
> Mr Hamilton was so kind as to present me to the King, who is to
> be of age in January next. He is but sixteen then. He is not very manly
> or tall of his age. He is not very handsome, but a good likeness to the
> Duke of York. He is not by all accounts the brightest of young men. He
> speaks no other language than Neapolitan, which is infamous Italian,
> but he does that by way of being popular ... But they are all very igno-
> rant, think of nothing but of crowding as many servants behind their
> coaches as it can well hold, two running footmen before and fine hors-
> es. You'll see them sometimes walking upon the quay with five or six
> servants and their coach following them.

Ferdinand IV, King of Naples, was now a boy of fifteen. When his
father went to Spain as Charles III in 1759 Ferdinand had succeeded
to the throne of Naples. Charles had done much for Naples by way
of political reform; and he had inaugurated a vast building pro-
gramme. He needed country palaces for the shooting and hunting of
which he was so fond; and as summer residences for his Court. Thus
arose the palace, gardens and cascades of Caserta; which was the
architect Vanvitelli's masterpiece; and which rivalled Versailles. Slaves

were employed – for the last time in Europe – in the building of the palace, which was so vast that it was still unfinished when Charles left Naples. It was not, in fact, completed until many years later. He also built the palace of Capodimonte. And in Naples itself Charles erected the splendid San Carlo Opera house.

The regency which his father had set up in 1759 when Ferdinand was eight was due to end shortly, when he came of age at sixteen in January 1767. The Regent Tanucci had continued Charles' reforms, but had neglected the education of the King; some said deliberately, in order to increase his own authority; others said because the boy's mind was incapable of bearing the strain of education. Ferdinand inherited his father's love of sport and his ram-like profile; but little else. He was unintelligent and uneducated. At this time, although he was already fifteen years old, his principal amusement was to play with puppets.

> The opera house here is magnificent beyond anything I ever saw. People take their boxes by the year, and you go and make your visits to them there. Nobody ever thinks of listening, except when there comes a favourite tune; then they are so attentive that you might hear a pin drop ...

The San Carlo opera house, at that time the largest and finest in the world,[*] was built in eight months in the year 1737, to the designs of Giovanni Antonio Medrano. On gala nights it was brilliantly lighted; in front of every box were candles reflected by looking-glasses. It was the centre of social life. As in every other opera house in Italy, the audience was badly behaved and talked throughout most of the performance. The King, uneducated like his subjects, would sit in the royal box eating macaroni with his fingers. Naples at this time was enjoying the fruits of the great age of her music; Scarlatti and Pergolese (La Serva Padrona) were to be followed by Cimarosa, now a young man of seventeen; Metastasio had supplied many of the libretti, while to its great Colleggi di Musica Naples owed her abundance of excellent singers.

Before William sat down again to write of his doings to his mother, another week had passed. The weather was like summer – 'one has one's windows open all day long, though close by the sea.' He had continued his social activities; and seen a lady take the veil:

* The Scala in Milan was not completed until 1778.

November 25th, 1766 ... The oddest fashion to me here is that of a lady, if she lose her mother or father or any near relation, she keeps open house for nine days; where everybody she is acquainted with goes and makes her a bow. She sits in a corner and looks dismal; and everybody sits about her, and talks to one another but not to her. It is also the fashion here for a lady to see company two days after she is brought to bed. The ladies breed here very fast – fourteen or fifteen children is not uncommon; which causes their being so many more nuns here than in most places.

I was yesterday to see a nun take the veil. One would have thought it a serious ceremony, but they make quite a farce of it. The women keep laughing the whole time and make such a noise that one would rather think one was at an opera than in a church. I am told it is much more serious in France. She sits before the altar while they perform mass, then she received the sacrament. When that is done she walks with a taper in her [hand] round the church into a chapel of the convent, where they take off all her finery and dress her like a nun. She comes to the grate, where the man that performs the mass takes a pair of scissors and cuts a lock of her hair and reads some little prayer. When that is done the nuns kiss her and cut her hair quite short. Then everybody goes to the gate of the convent which opened for all the nuns to make their appearance and the poor nun takes leave of her acquaintances.

And so the days passed agreeably enough. Balls, concerts, dinners, the opera, evenings with Mr Hamilton, mornings looking at 'curiosities' – William enjoyed it all.

Meanwhile, Lady Holland and the rest of her family had been making what William called her 'monstrous journey' over the Alps. At Chambéry she had been joined by Ste and Lady Mary. She had crossed the Mont Cenis in an open chair, carried by men for hours at a time up and down rocks upon which it seemed impossible for anything but goats to walk. Often she was within a hair's breadth of 'the most frightful' precipices, and she was hardly comforted by the men's assurance that there was no danger. Going up the mountain the cold had been almost unbearable; on the top and coming down there had been rain and fog. When she finally took courage and peeped out of her chair, 'the sight was indeed glorious', though the fog prevented her from seeing all the beauty of it. Her carriage was dismantled and carried over by mules, and was reassembled on the other side; mules loaded with silk and other goods continually passed and repassed along this route between Lyons and Turin. The party arrived at Turin on 28 October. From here, a fatiguing journey of seven days brought them to Florence, to the '*sweets of Arno's vale, la bella Italia, le centre des beaux arts et du goût*'. The road had led them through Milan, Piacenza, Parma and Modena to Bologna, where they met Francis Andrews, Provost of Trinity College, Dublin, who complained heavily that in the midst of vineyards he could not get a good glass of wine.

'When we left Bologna, which is a day and a half from this town,' wrote Lady Holland from Florence, 'we began to cross the Appenines and the scene all along is beautiful; numbers of villas and beautiful buildings, with groves of cypress trees and falls of water ... The Appenines, tho' high mountains, after the Alps appear nothing.'

Ste and his mother diverted themselves with discovering French chimney pieces, many of which were copied in almost every Italian town. Mr Upton looked after the party – it was his tenth visit to Italy. Little Harry Fox rode beside the carriage, perfectly happy except when he met with a bad horse.

At Florence Lady Holland stayed at an inn which looked out on the river, a charming prospect of 'two beautiful bridges'. She went to a *conversazione* at Sir Horace Mann's – which she did not enjoy. She thought the women looked vulgar and stupid, and found them hard to talk to. However, she left Florence with regret. The environs she considered quite enchanting: 'orange groves, Catalonian jasmine hedges growing out in the gardens, and all the hills and sides of the hills cover'd with villas, cypresses, firs, and the most beautiful buildings ... it really resembles what one reads in story-books and fairytales.'

After four tiring days on the road, Lady Holland and her party arrived at Rome. They entered the city by moonlight, with their landau open.

On 27 November Lady Holland arrived at Naples. William was delighted to hear about their long journey; especially how in Rome they had been to see their cousins, the Young Pretender and the Cardinal of York. 'Lady Holland and Charles are dreadful J[acobit]es', William informed his mother. 'Bonnie Prince Charlie' and his brother, living then in exile in Italy, were cousins of both William and the Foxes, through their common ancestor, Charles I;

Charles II's son by Louise de Kérouaille was the first Duke of Richmond, grandfather of William's mother and of Lady Holland.

William now heard that his father had just been created Duke of Leinster. This gave William himself the courtesy title of Marquess of Kildare. He was delighted; he closed a letter with the words, 'KILDARE I may venture to sign'.

The days were filled with bright sunshine. William could sit by his open window, looking out on the sea and at Mount Vesuvius:

> December 9th, 1766. The climate here is, to be sure, charming. I am now sitting with my windows open and no fire. We have no fire in any of the rooms, and I do not suppose we shall have any this winter, as they say this is the coldest weather we shall have. The Neapolitan people complain of its being cold, and the gentlemen and ladies have all got their muffs and fur cloaks. The gentlemen of the *bon ton* have their muffs; I believe I shall get myself one for to be in the fashion, more than for the use.
>
> I was yesterday to see a palace belonging to the King, called Capua de Monte. The King never lives there as there are neither chairs nor tables, but there is a great many fine pictures and more bad ones. I was also to see the day before yesterday, the *Grotto del Cane*, which you may have heard of. I had the experiment tried of holding the dog's nose upon the ground, and it takes away his breath and is taken out in all appearance dead, and as soon as you put him in the air he recovers. I had often heard that it was not cruel, as the dog suffered no pain; but I think it is the most cruel thing I ever saw, as the dog is in all the agonies of death. There also is, close by the Grotto del Cane, a most beautiful lake; it is surrounded by hills charmingly planted; the lake is covered with wild fowl of all sorts; the King shoots there very often.

The Palace of Capodimonte had been designed by Medrano – the architect of the San Carlo opera house. Here King Charles had come to shoot *beccafichi*. But its fame rested, of course, on the porcelain factory that Charles had established there in 1743. In 1759 he destroyed the furnaces and took the factory with him to Spain, where he re-established it at Buen Retiro.

By the middle of December the weather had broken; every day it poured with rain. William was hoping to get a bit of lava from Vesuvius for his brother Charles in Ireland; not a finely polished piece, but one 'just as it comes from the mountain ... next time I go, if I can I will get him a bit that I have seen red hot'. At this time the mountain burnt very little; what fire he saw was very deep in the mountain. Ste Fox had been so badly bitten on the legs by gnats that he had to be carried up and down the three flights of stairs of their house. 'It is ridiculous to see him in the chair, for he sits with so much *grandeur* that he makes himself a few pounds more than if he was to sit in the common way.'

William did not neglect his studies. He rode and fenced every day. He was having lessons in Italian, although his Italian master was a 'very stupid one'. There was no good dancing master, but he was able to find an engineer to teach him fortification and drawing, a man who seemed to have a good method of teaching. In addition to his education, William had social obligations to fulfil. One of the most important aspects of these being his dress, he now found himself 'obliged to make a fine coat for the King's birthday here the 12th of January, as everything is to be magnificent on account of his being of age'. To pay for this coat he drew more than £60. 'It is a very handsome velvet; I cannot explain it well, but it is handsome and fine, though not tawdry. It is a little too grave for me, but that becomes fat people best.'

Lady Holland had decided it was necessary to have a *conversazione* once a week: 'she begins next Thursday, which the people here are very glad of.' Already many Italian ladies had been to see her, and she was anxious to return their civilities. 'Lady Holland's *conversazione* was very brilliant on Thursday last,' wrote William a few days later. But Lady Holland was happiest when with her own family. The mornings they spent 'airing' and dined at three o'clock, which was late for Naples; they went for drives into the country; they supped 'always *en famille* at ten exactly and keep good hours'. William almost always came home to supper at ten with her; and if he did not, she knew where he was. He had more to do than he had time for; he took great pains to improve himself in everything; every minute of his time from seven in the morning was employed either in diverting himself or in learning something.

And so Christmas with its festivities arrived:

December 26th, 1766 ... I was Christmas eve in several of the churches. I was much disappointed, as I expected to have seen a much finer procession and better music, all the churches better lighted. I was at one of the best, where they performed High Mass. After they had done, they carried our Saviour in procession round the church, and then put him in a manger that was built up on purpose for that occasion, where there was a number of puppets dressed like shepherds, and the Virgin Mary and Joseph. The procession was attended by the monks of the convent; they got common music out of the street for to play before the procession, though there was a very fine band music in the church. After our Saviour was laid in the manger, it really was quite a puppet show as that common music stood playing there, drunk.

I have also been to see some of the presepes, which are really worth seeing. There is our Saviour lying in a manger, and the Virgin Mary and Joseph, and the shepherds. There is the people from all nations coming to see him. It is the most natural thing I ever saw. You see hills and rivers, rocks, cattle grazing, people; you would think it was nature itself as it is so well imitated. At one of them there was hills which one could hardly believe they were not real hills that one saw; I hardly thought that the human eye could be so deceived.

The 'Presepe', or representation of the Nativity, was an established form of art in Naples. The best masters of the day were employed to make the figures, which were of carved wood or terracotta and dressed in Neapolitan costumes. The gifts of the Magi might be of finely worked gold and silver. The great families vied with one another to possess the best figures, sometimes spending as much as £1,500 or £2,000 on a Presepe. Sometimes they were set out on the flat roofs of the houses, where they looked picturesque against the view of Vesuvius and the bay.

The city was at this time full of visitors. 'Naples,' wrote William, 'is very agreeable. The misfortune of it is there is too many English. Amongst the rest there is the Provost here.' The Provost of Trinity College, Dublin, Francis Andrews, whom Lady Holland had met at Bologna, was a remarkable man. Six years previously, at a cost of £11,000, he had built the Provost's house, adjoining Trinity College. Designed by an Irish architect, it is said to have been modelled on a house built in Piccadilly by Lord Burlington. Under Andrews the west front of Trinity was completed, and most of Parliament Square was built. He encouraged learning at the University, founding the chairs of Mathematics and Hebrew and separating the chair of Modern History from that of Oratory; in his will be provided for the endowment of an astronomical observatory. He sat in the Irish Parliament for his native Derry. He lived abroad a good deal for reasons of health. His wit and knowledge made him an agreeable companion. At Padua the professors were greatly impressed by the fluency with which he addressed them in Latin and by his other scholarly accomplishments.

'A merry Xmas and a happy New Year to my dearest sister and all her fire-side,' wrote Lady Holland to the Duchess of Leinster on New Year's day, 1767. And so the new year dawned. 'We have no fire-side,' she continued, 'but the sun so hot in the middle of the day we sit with our windows open, only think of that at this time of the year.' Lord Holland was as well as he could hope to be. Sitting in the warm clear sunshine he came to the conclusion that his ill-health was due simply to old age.

A week later William was writing that it had rained for the past four days, and that he had been obliged to have a little fire, more for the damp than the cold:

> January 6th, 1767 ... Naples continues very agreeable. I amuse myself very well. The carnival begins the latter end of next week. I believe I shall be a little tired of it before it is over, as it is very long this year. As I have told you how well I amused myself, it is time to mention how I employ myself. I ride and fence every day; three times a week I study fortifications and draw plans. The other three times I have my Italian master, who is a very good one; he does not speak French or English; I have had but a few *leçons* of him and I am much improved. At first when I came I had a master but he understood French and English so well, that he would always talk English or French; during that time I did not improve in the least. For my fortification and drawing master is a very good one; he is an engineer in this service, and reckoned a very good one, draws very well. I have taken but a few *leçons*, and this day drawn the plan of my two rooms. He is publishing the *Antiquities of Sicily*, which I hope to see. May I venture to subscribe for you or the Duke? It is but five guineas for four volumes. I have enquired into the man's character, and everybody gives him a good character ...
>
> The King comes of age next Monday; they say he has given orders to the gentleman in waiting to wake him as soon as the clock strikes twelve on Sunday night. I believe he is mistaken a little, as his power will not be great as he imagines while his father lives; as by what I hear there is a regular account sent to Spain of everything he does, be it ever so trifling – even the days he goes out of shooting and of what he kills and of what kind ...
>
> Pray look at my seal. It is an antique out of Lady Mary's collection.

King Ferdinand's first act after his minority ended was the expulsion of the Jesuits. But he was a weak king, and after his marriage the following year to Maria Carolina of Austria he came entirely under her influence. She it was who broke Tanucci's power, and caused his dismissal some years later.

In the meantime the King was determined that his coming of age should be attended with all possible splendour. William describes how he went to Court on the King's Birthday:

> January 19th, 1767 ... I was at Court, where I saw all the people kissing his hand one after another as fast as they could*; I believe I saw very near a hundred. And I believe as many more before I came. In the evening he went to the opera, which was illuminated upon the occasion, and the number of people, and such a deal of finery made a prodigious brilliant appearance. There was a great number of fine clothes, but very few pretty ones.

Meanwhile, the Carnival had begun. 'The Carnival,' wrote William, 'begun the day before yesterday. I have not found the difference yet between Carnival time or other time. But by next post I dare say I shall.' The amount of money he had been obliged to spend was a constant source of worry to him. He had already drawn hundreds of pounds, and he now found he would soon have to draw more. His birthday coat alone had come to £63. He found it best to pay cash for everything; in this way the people, who loved to see the money, let him have things cheaper. 'My dear Mother,' wrote the worried young man, 'I can assure you I take particular care to be as little extravagant as it is possible, and Bolle's accounts are very regular and exact.' At any rate William had no desire to take part in the excessive gambling that went on in the city. But to the temptation of works of art he was more vulnerable. 'There is a book of Etruscan vases printed here and projected by Mr Hamilton; a great number of pretty things in it; the subscription comes to about 8 guineas.' The book in question was *Antiquités etrusques, grecques et romaines*, (4 vols. Naples, 1766-7). Josiah Wedgwood was much influenced by the plates representing Hamilton's vases in this book, and imitated them in his designs.

The weather had been so bad for several weeks that it had been impossible for William to stir to see any of the curiosities about Naples; but towards the end of the month it improved, and the party

---

* Casanova says that when he kissed the boy's hand at a Court function it was covered with chilblains.

was able to do some sightseeing. Charles Fox and Lord Holland had been writing to George Selwyn, promising to get him something out of Herculaneum.*

> January 27th, 1767 ... I was yesterday to see a great many antiquities such as temples and buildings, etc. I was in the Elysian fields, where there was a great many ancient tombs. I was also at Nero's baths, which are very curious. They are under ground, one is obliged to go naked, otherways one could not sustain the heat. I went on quite to the end where the water was nearly boiling hot, so much that I could not put my finger in it. I had also an egg boil in it and I never ate a better one. I was obliged to carry a torch in my hand; so you may guess what a pretty figure I was coming out. We went through a great many underground passages, which were extremely curious. Amongst the rest we went to Agrippa's tomb, which is very curious; the fine stucco work so well finished was delightful to the eyes.
>
> We was in Sybil's grotto, which is prodigious large. We dined close to a temple of Juno's. After dinner we went to a mountain, which they called Monte Novo. It has been a volcano, which they pretend to say was thrown up in one night: it is certainly very curious. We were at a temple of Syrapis, which is the most curious thing I saw; for it is in direct shape. It was supported by marble pillars, three of which are standing. They are of a good height and I should take them to be about 20 foot high. I measured the diameter on one that was down which was about 4 feet 3 inches.
>
> Saturday last I was with Lord Holland to see the King's museum at Portici, which is one of his palaces about 5 miles from Naples, where there is all the things that were found at Herculaneum. There is a great many statues, vases, etc., etc., all in bronze. There is also a whole set of kitchen furniture; a great many things that we have to this day, such as copper pans, for cheese cakes, etc. There is a little copper saucepan lined with silver. There is two loaves of bread that was found, some wine which is turned into pitch. There is oil which they say smells well. In short, there is so many curious things there that it is impossible to remember them all, it is a thing that must be seen often.

The discovery of Herculaneum is a romantic story. During the War of the Spanish Succession the Austrian army advanced through Italy taking many of the Spanish possessions. With the Austrians came the

---

* See CJ Fox to Selwyn, Marseilles, Oct. 31 [1766]; CJ Fox to Selwyn, Naples Nov. 21 [1766]; and Lord Holland to Selwyn, Naples, Dec. 2 [1766]. These three letters are wrongly dated 1769 in Jesse's *George Selwyn and his Contemporaries*.

Prince d'Elboeuf, a cousin of Prince Eugène. He held an army command and was posted to Naples. He spent the summer of 1710 in a villa at Portici. Subsequently he heard that a farmer, in deepening his well, had discovered pieces of columns and marble. D'Elboeuf bought the site, continued the digging, brought up more statues, and discovered, far underground, a vast building. He built himself a villa at Portici in which to place his finds. Meanwhile the best of these, three white marble draped female figures, he sent as a present to Prince Eugène in Vienna. But d'Elboeuf was often called away by duty, so he eventually sold his villa, and excavations ceased. When Prince Eugène died his niece inherited the three marble women, which she sold to Augustus III, Elector of Saxony and King of Poland. The story now moves to Charles III, King of Naples. Charles married Augustus III's daughter, Maria Amalia Christina, who no doubt knew the history of her father's three marble women. Shortly after Charles was proclaimed King of the Two Sicilies, he went to Portici to fish. D'Elboeuf's villa was available, so he bought it. When he entered the house he was amazed and delighted to find it full of the antique marbles which the prince had left behind. He decided to continue the excavations. And his wife, whom he married in 1738, greatly encouraged him. Amongst the first discoveries was an inscription which proved that the vast building which d'Elboeuf had come upon some twenty years previously was in fact the Theatre of Herculaneum.

The impact on the world of 1738 of the news that Herculaneum – lost for sixteen centuries – had been found must have been resounding – Pompeii was not identified until 25 years later.*

> Carnival has been begun some time but I have not found out the difference yet between it and other times; but tonight the first balls begin which is only for the nobility, but they invite all strangers. But the officers give balls where the second nobility comes, which I am told are the most agreeable. You must know that the first nobility goes to their balls but won't let them come to theirs, which I think is hard.

William enjoyed the ball; and a few days later he was writing:

> 3rd of February ... We are to have another ball tonight. The last was

---

* See Professor Charles Seltman's interesting article 'A Mine of Statues' in *History Today*, January 1951.

agreeable enough; it was not crowded; but there was none but the first
nobility. Join [*sic*] is a subscription made by the first people here and
they won't admit of any but the first rank and there is but few of them
dance. They let hairdressers and their wives and milliners come sooner
than the second nobility. Most of the ladies came in black dominoes,
without masks. The gentlemen came dressed as usual, the milliners etc.
etc. come in masks into the room and then they pull them off for dancing. There is a supper which is very well conducted; people make their
own parties, but it does not begin till past 2 o'clock. There is great
hopes of a masquerade ball at the great opera house, which must be a
fine sight, as everybody is let in that pays 3 or 4 shillings, and the house
is able to contain about five thousand people.

Devoted to his mother, the Duchess of Leinster, William was
delighted with the present Lady Holland had just given him: a snuff
box with the Duchess' portrait on it. 'I can assure you,' he told her,
'every time I look at it it gives me pleasure to think I have you in
my pocket.'

One of the greatest attractions of Naples, to tourists, was, of
course, Vesuvius. So far the volcano had been fairly quiet, but
William lived in hopes of seeing an eruption. Mr Hamilton, who
took a great interest in the mountain, thought it very likely that there
would soon be one. 'I hope,' said William, 'if it would do no mischief
that it may be a great one, as it would be a fine sight.' At night it
showed up well: 'I am in great hopes that we are going to have an
eruption of Mount Vesuvius, for it threatens very much. There is a
great deal of fire coming out of the top every night; it is a prodigious
fine sight and I have a fine view out of my window of it.'

A few days later things started to liven up: Mount Vesuvius makes a
great noise and flings up a great deal of matter; I am still in hopes of
having an eruption ... Pray tell the Duke there has been a little shock of
an earthquake, but I did not feel it.

And, later:

There has been violent shocks of earthquakes at Genoa, but as yet they
have escaped this place. I must own I should like just to feel a little one,
that would do no harm; but I am afraid at this present time an earthquake would be of bad consequence to Naples, as a great part of this
town is in a very tottering condition; there has been one or two houses

tumble down since I have been here. Our house is very safe as it is built upon a rock, or else it would be in some danger, having two such monsters as Ste and I in it.

But William was to be disappointed: no great eruption took place, nor did he feel an earthquake, during his stay in Naples.

The Carnival dancing went on, but – 'fewer balls than has ever been known. The excuse is it is so long; but last year it was short, there was not a night but there were three or four.' There was, after all, to be no masquerade at the opera, 'which is a great pity, as it must have been a fine sight'. However, William saw one of the regular features of the Carnival, the *Cuccagna*, which dated from Spanish days. He disliked it intensely:

> February the 10th, 1767 ... There is a very curious sight the four last Sundays of Carnival, which is called the *Cochania*; it is a scaffolding that is built up before the King's palace, where there is all sorts of provisions hung on it, such as beef, mutton and veal and bread. It is surrounded by soldiers; and when the Captain General gives the signal they let in the mob, which is very numerous; as there is not only the mob of the town, which is I believe one of the greatest in Europe, but those of the town [sic]; Last Sunday was a bad day, so there was not so many as was expected; but in a quarter of an hour they don't leave a bit. It is, I suppose, the greatest encouragement of idleness, cruelty and wickedness that can possibly be thought of, as it generally ends in a great number of them being stabbed. I am told at the next Sunday there is to be live creatures, that are to be nailed up and to be torn to pieces by the mob.

William was still waiting to hear whether his father, the Duke, wished to subscribe for the book of Etruscan vases:

> 24th of February... I mentioned in a former letter a book of Etruscan vases printed here by subscription, under the direction of Mr Hamilton. I have not yet subscribed, as I waited for an answer. But as the time of my departure draws near, I hope the Duke will not disapprove of my subscribing. It is about ten guineas, and it will be a very good ornament to the library, and a pleasant book to dip into, as there is very pretty figures, and vases to draw from. It'll also oblige Mr Hamilton, who has been very civil to me.

William had by now at last been drawn into the gambling. The money he drew from his bankers, a hundred pounds at a time, he handed over to Mr Bolle to pay his expense. Many of his letters are headed by Mr Bolle's receipt, such as the following:

NAPLES, the 3rd of March, 1767. Received of the Marquess of Kildare, the sum of five hundred and twenty ducates*; or ninety-seven pounds, ten shillings sterling, for which I am to be accountable by me. A. BOLLE.*

William hastened to excuse himself for his apparent extravagance:

3rd of March, 1767. My dearest Mother, I am ashamed to trouble you with the above receipt. I am afraid that it goes out rather too fast, but I am sure that Bolle's accounts are very exact. I believe that it has slipped a little too fast through my fingers. Mrs Hamilton, our Minister's wife, you must know plays at loo, and at first she could get nobody to make her party. I used, against my will, to be set down to it. At that time they played very low. But latterly Ste Fox and Lady Mary chose to make it deeper, and I generally lost, so that I am out of pocket in all 30 or 40 pounds. But latterly I have not played at all, so that I am in hopes their party flourishes without me.

Driving about the environs of Naples with the Hollands, William saw the pretty peasant girls in their picturesque dresses. Lady Holland has left us a description. On holidays, she observed, there was a great mixture of ancient and eastern dress, 'some very like those of the Greek islands in the *cent estampes*'. They wore white veils, the hair drawn back and beaded with bodkins, or plaited, like that of ancient busts. The dress was eastern; no stays but close waistcoats laced with gold lacing; loose jackets of black velvet, scarlet cloth, and various other colours richly laced, some of them with gold; gold chains about their necks and gold earrings. Some had milk-white waistcoats, white veils, and a white petticoat with a border embroidered in worsteds of various colours. The people of fashion dressed in the French and English style, better than the latter, not so well as the former, except that they did not wear 'that odious rouge'. The middle-class people were 'sad tawdry figures'; French, English and their own dress all mixed together, making a very ugly appearance.

Lady Holland later describes her visit to Pompeii four years after it had been identified. She saw the remains of a small temple, a soldiers'

---

* The ducat of Naples was worth three shillings and nine pence.

barracks, a street and a private house; 'but,' she wrote, 'the simpletons throw the earth back again, and don't go on when they come to what they imagine was a private house, which is provoking, as one should have infinite more curiosity to see that than any public building'.

Although William was not in love, he was a 'general flirt', and loved by all.* He was particularly fond of his cousin, the Countess Mahony, and for this reason was much teased by Lady Holland and her family. 'Lord Kildare and his cousin Mahony,' said Lady Holland, 'are very great indeed; she is wonderfully fond of him, she must be fifty years old, but a very well looking woman of her age, *de l'embonpoint de la fraîcheur*. She is really drôle and entertaining.' And again, 'We have fine fun about Lord Kildare and his old cousin, who is wonderfully fond of him.' Lady Holland loved William dearly. 'I never knew,' she wrote, 'a more obliging good-natured attentive disposition than his. He is not the least shy with regard to making acquaintance, for he knows all Naples; but he is diffident, which I like him the better for. He improves in his person, and takes proper pains not to grow fat, by fencing, walking, and riding at the riding-house; indeed, my sweet siss, I think he goes on just as you would both wish him to do.'

The time of William's departure from Naples was now drawing near. For several weeks he had been planning ahead:

> You'll be so kind as to ask il Signor Duca whether I am to have letters of credit from Mr Nesbit, as I have none to Rome or elsewhere in Italy. I suppose from this I shall go to Rome, to Florence and to Venice. I mean to go to Venice in May if the Duke has no objections, for to see the Doge marry the Adriatick, which I am told is a very fine procession and worth seeing. And as Venice is worth seeing it will be killing two birds with one stone. And it is a very stupid place except in Carnival and at that time, I am told.

The custom of wedding the Adriatic with a ring thrown from a ship was introduced by the Doge Sebastian Ziani in the twelfth century; the ceremony took place on Ascension Day.

> One of your letters mentioning that the Duke saying I had time enough to see everything, so that I shall stay a good while at places that is worth seeing. Florence and Turin I dare say I shall like vastly. At Rome one

* Lady Catherine Annesley had by this time married a Mr Toole, 'a cadet in some of the French troops; a bad match in point of fortune'.

may spend one's morning very well by visiting the curiosities which are in abundance, which is amusing enough. But other ways it is very dull, as this Pope has forbid all kinds of amusements.

The Pope who had 'forbid all kinds of amusements' was Clement XIII; his attempts to support the Jesuit missionaries were largely unsuccessful, and before his death they had been expelled from Naples, Spain, Portugal and France.

Amongst the places William wanted to visit was Pisa, to see the ceremony of the Battle of the Bridge, 'which everybody thinks worth while seeing, as it is a thing that happens but once in a great number of years.' The Grand Duke of Tuscany was to be there, 'and all the world ...'

The Carnival ended on 3 March with two balls:

One is the subscription ball that I have mentioned in one of my former letters. The other is at the Prince Francavilla, which is a masquerade ball. He gave four this Carnival. I was at two of them. The last there was about 1600 tickets delivered out, and I believe tonight there'll be 100 or 2 more. It is a very fine sight, as it is a noble house.

And so the Neapolitan festivities came to an end; William prepared for his departure. Ste Fox and Lady Mary had already left, 'to make a little tour of Italy before they return'. The middle of March saw Lady Holland and Charles take the road for Rome; the road that she had on her outward journey described thus: 'Only think of there being now a marshy desert place between this [Naples] and Rome, where once there stood twenty-four great cities, now only some ruins here and there'. The following day, 17 March, Lord Holland wrote: 'I am just stepping into my chaise for Rome.' William himself remained in Naples a few more days before following the Hollands to the Papal city.

3

ROME

Driving along the Via Appia from Naples that March day, 1767, the view of the city gradually receded, and, looking back, William saw for the last time the grand outlines of Vesuvius. Eventually that, too, was lost to sight, and the carriage lurched along the road through the Campanian plain. The road was appalling, the inns worse. At every stop beggars crowded round the carriage, crying out for alms. Indeed, the character of these southern people was maintained right up to the frontier of the Kingdom of the Two Sicilies. At the border William went through the customs formalities; once across, he was in the Papal States. The famous Appian Way, with its magnificent views of sea, mountains and sky, continued past the gulf of Gaeta and Formia; past the place where Cicero lived, and the beach on which he died at the orders of Mark Antony and Augustus; the Pontine Marshes; the ruins of Roman villas; here an ancient tomb, there a rugged castle of a white village on a hill; groves of Roman pines; and the broken arches of Roman aqueducts endlessly spanning the countryside.

Driving across the sad, bleak Campagna, William watched the long lines of the ruined aqueducts, all converging onto the same focal point: a cluster of cupolas glinting in the sun. The driver looked round to William, and, pointing with his whip towards the dome of St Peter's, shouted: *Ecco Roma!*

Rome was a place of gardens and parks and palaces; of lovely smells and sounds; of flowers and flowering shrubs; of birds singing and water falling from many fountains; of great palaces built of cut stone, with iron grilles over their lower windows; of tall buildings covered with the typical rich golden-brown plaster; of the washing of the poor fluttering on a line at the foot of some ancient classical ruin; of fallen columns and broken statues still shrouded by green trees and undergrowth and centuries of silted earth; of black or scarlet clothed priests, of sandalled monks and voluminous-skirted nuns; of elegant princes and tattered paupers; of a pope who called himself *Pontifex Maximus* and who wore the imperial purple; of cardinals who combined celibacy with fornication; of narrow streets and domed, baroque churches. And it was the capital of the worst-governed of all the states of Italy.

William had been in Rome only a few days when he received letters from home indicating that his father for some reason wished him to return to Naples. But the boy was fast growing to be a man, to know his own mind, and to act upon it:

> ROME, April the 4th, 1767 ... I hope the Duke does not take it ill my not returning to Naples immediately. In the first place, I have a violent breaking out in my face and foot, so that a journey would have been disagreeable. In the next place, I thought after so long a journey that the Duke would not be displeased at my staying to see the functions that are performed here in the holy week. But in a few days after I shall return according to your desires.

As we shall see, William did not in fact return to Naples; he stayed in Rome till June, when he went to Florence.

Holy Week at Rome drew vast crowds of English tourists. Already all the Englishmen who had been in Naples had arrived in Rome, which by no means made the latter place more agreeable. With everyone going to see the same sights, and generally lodging in the same quarter* of the city, it was hard to avoid one's fellow countrymen. But it was by no means necessary to associate only with these people; even to the ordinary Grand Tourist the Romans were renowned for their hospitality; and a nobleman of William's rank could count on finding most of the princely doors thrown open to him. Nugent in his guide book, *The Grand Tour* describes how 'noblemen of the first rank, both secular and ecclesiastic, who, upon hearing a traveller at their gate desirous of seeing the curiosities of their palaces will take pleasure in showing them themselves; and, if they happen to be busy, order their domestics to do it for them, leaving their cabinets to give strangers liberty to satisfy their curiosity'.

---

* Although William does not tell us where he stayed, merely heading his letters 'Rome' and the date, the fashionable quarter for foreigners was the Piazza di Spagna and the streets leading from it. Here were the coffee-houses, taverns, banks and shops frequented by Englishmen. The ambassador of Spain at Rome exercised a royal jurisdiction in the Piazza di Spagna and in the neighbourhood, which became for that reason the safest and quietest quarters of the city.

With so much of beauty and historic interest to be seen, William lost no time in beginning the serious work of sightseeing. He continued his letter of 4 April:

> I am very much pleased with what I have seen here. I have spent 3 hours every morning in going to see *Palazze* and churches, etc., etc. Their house, or rather, as they call them, *palazzo*, are very noble but very uncomfortable. They inhabit a few rooms; the rest are open for the world to come and see. And, to be sure, you see a noble suite of rooms furnished with a number of fine pictures, statues, busts, etc., mostly antique.
>
> Their villas are beautiful, but the houses are uncomfortable in general. The villas are well furnished with antiquities. Most of them have been built by cardinals, for generally the cardinals that are of no great family built a *palazzo* and a villa for his heirs, let them be ever so poor and not able to support it after his death.
>
> I forget if I mentioned it in Emily's letter, but I had the honour of kissing the pope's toe. (N.B. *it was very sweet.*) He is a very agreeable old man and is very fond of having the strangers presented to him.

One hundred years earlier Evelyn described in his Diary his visit to the pope: 'I was presented to kiss his toe, that is, his embroidered slipper, two cardinals holding up his vest and surplice: and then, being sufficiently blessed with his thumb and two fingers for that day, I returned home to dinner.' Papal pomp in the eighteenth century was brilliant. The streets through which the Pope passed were the only ones kept clean. Everywhere he went the streets were strewn with green, all the bells were rung, and everyone knelt to receive his blessing, not rising until he had passed. Those who did not wish to kneel or to descend from their carriages were compelled to go into another street. The Church encouraged tourists because they enriched the city by expending great sums of money there annually.

> I am afraid during my stay here my correspondence will not be quite so regular as I could wish, as, what with my masters and what with antiquity hunting, my morning will be a good deal taken up. As soon as my forehead is well I shall attend the *conversazione*. As yet I have only been to one, which was the Princess Altieri, who is sister to the Princess Francavilla, who I have mentioned from Naples. She was so kind as to give me a letter to her. As the Italians are very proud, they like people should bring them letters. The Turin minister gave me 5 against I go to Turin. If I had not received Emily's letter my intention was to have

delayed the Venice jaunt and to have stayed here till the middle of June
... and to have gone to Florence where I intended making a long stay. I
had never any thoughts of going with Lord and Lady Holland, as I am
of your opinion in making a long stay at the places where I find agreeable. I must own as much as I like Naples in winter I believe it would
be far from agreeable in summer. I am very lucky in having the
Countess of Mahony and her daughter here, as they are very civil to me,
which will make my time very agreeable here. I am rather glad that I do
not go to Venice this year, as all the English that are here at present go
there directly after the holy week.

The Hollands had by this time left Rome, and were staying in
Florence. They were, in fact, on their way home to England, which
they reached towards the end of May, preceded by Ste and Lady
Mary. Charles Fox remained on in Italy.

The Countess Mahony, we remember, had been very friendly
with William at Naples. Her daughter had married Benedetto,
Prince Giustiniani. The Giustinianis were a very old Roman family, descended, they said, from the Emperor Justinian. They had left
Naples a few days before William, and had come to Rome, where
the Giustinianis lived. They proposed that William should come
with them, but William declined, preferring to stay on in Naples a
little while longer. Now they were all happy to meet again in Rome.
William was, after all, through Countess Mahony, their cousin, and
was delighted to be in their company. We learn from Lady Holland
that Princess Giustiniani was one of the best bred and most agreeable of the Italian ladies; she had no *cicisbeo*, and was attached to her
husband and her children, of which she had seven. In Rome she was
much loved and respected. The Roman ladies were rather better
educated than the Neapolitans; and Countess Mahony, who was a
sensible woman, sent her daughter to a convent in Rome in preference to keeping her at Naples. But Rome might have been a disagreeable place for English ladies to live in, because the pride and
etiquette, which was tiresome among all Italians, was more there
than anywhere else.

There are here, [continued William], two famous portrait painters. The
one you have often heard of; his name is Pompeio Battoni. The other
is one Maron, a German (*sic*) who is much cheaper – some people reck-
on much better. I have seen some of his pictures, which are very like ...
I have sent a box with some lava, snuff boxes, and a bit of different sort

of stuff that comes out of Vesuvius for Charles. They went with Lord Holland's things by sea. If you think proper to send for them over to Ireland, you'll be so good as to divide them between you.

Pompeo Girolamo Batoni had been born at Lucca and was the son of a goldsmith. He had made a great name for himself in Rome, his only rival being Mengs. Anton von Maron was an Austrian.

Holy Week, with its church ceremonies, came, and William was glad to be in Rome to see them:

> April the 15th, 1767 ... Tomorrow begin the great functions in the churches. The Pope is to bless his Catholicks, and to excommunicate us poor hereticks, and to wash the feet of the pilgrims. The Cardinals all dine together at St Peter's, which is, to be sure, a noble building. I was this evening at the Pope's chapel to hear them chant their evening service; the Cardinals were all there. I have not yet seen the Cardinal York, but his brother I see every day. He has just quitted his mourning, and has given his servants our King's livery.

'James III' had died the previous year, and the young Pretender now called himself King of England. In spite of the efforts made on his behalf by his influential brother, the Cardinal of York, he was never recognised as King by the Pope; he had to be satisfied with the self-bestowed title of Count of Albany. He was now 47 years old, and a very different man from the dashing 'Bonnie Prince Charlie'. He was embittered, and given to 'the nasty bottle' – a practice which eventually killed him. The Cardinal was a much better man: kindly, dignified, and devout. His position brought him an annual income of £40,000.

> The Pope, [continued William] when in his robes in church is very like an old woman; he looked like a very cross one today, for he had just received an account of the King of Spain's banishing the Jesuits out of his dominions in Europe and America, etc.

One of the most enlightened despots in a despotic age, Charles III – a lean, untidy man with a large nose and intelligent eyes – was busy with reforms in Spain as he had been busy at Naples during his reign there. He made the Spaniards adopt sanitary reforms; he caused roads and canals to be constructed; he checked the power of the Church, reduced the number of monasteries and destroyed the Society of

Jesus. The Pope may well have looked like a very cross old woman. But what the Vatican and its servants suffered in dominions beyond their control was apparently amply compensated for in Rome. Protestant services were excluded from the Holy City, and those who wished to worship according to the Protestant faith had to proceed to a church outside the Porta del Popolo. In conversations touching upon religion heretics had to weigh their words; papal spies abounded, ready to report the expression of an unorthodox opinion, and to recommend the expulsion of the offender from the city within 24 hours on pain of inquisitorial imprisonment.

William had been unwilling to go to parties as long as the rash on his face remained; he contented himself with sightseeing and with attending the church ceremonies of Holy Week. By now the rash had disappeared, and he was anxious to go into society:

> April the 25th, 1767 ... My time begins to be more agreeable to me here, for, my face being well, the Princess Giustiniani is to introduce me to the best assemblies. Though not very agreeable things, I think it a good custom to use oneself to go into publick. The English begin to thin very fast; the latter of next [sic] there'll be half a dozen left out of the 40 that were here the other day.
>
> I am tomorrow morning to go to be introduced to the Cardinal Piccolomini, who is the most sensible man in Rome. To go to a Cardinal is like going to a Prince of the blood; as when the Pope gives them the red hat he tells them they rank with Kings and take place of Princes. My poor friend, the Pope, is out of spirits about the Jesuits, who are ordered out of Spain and every day expected. From which, if done, will be the greatest cut they have met with yet, as the estates of most of their colleges here at Rome are in the Kingdom of Naples.

Cardinal Enea Silvio Piccolomini, a member of a noble Sienese family which claimed to trace descent from Romulus, was Governor of Rome. He was 58 years old, and died the following year. He came from the same family as his more famous namesake, Enea Silvio de Piccolomini, known in literature as Aeneas Silvius, and who, as Pius II, was pope for six years during the fifteenth century. The expulsion of the Jesuits from the Bourbon territories was causing the Pope much distress. It will be recalled that Ferdinand, King of Naples' first act after reaching his majority in January of this year was their expulsion from the Kingdom of the Two Sicilies. No doubt he acted under the influence of his father. France had already expelled them; and the

Bourbon court of Parma followed suit.

With his entry into the exclusive Roman society, William found it necessary to provide himself with more finery. 'I am afraid,' he wrote, 'I shall be obliged to draw for money to get myself some *utensils of life*, as I am almost ragged in regard to linen'. Through the kindness of the gracious Princess Giustiniani he was now well launched into the life of the first nobility; his observations on this existence are acid:

> May the 2nd, 1767. I found by Emily's* last letter of the 26th of March that you and the Duke were not so desirous of my returning to Naples. I hope you have received my last of the 25th of April, wherein I mentioned my reasons for not returning; my face being very near well I begin to go more into company. I can't say I think their *conversazioni* the most agreeable I ever was in ... I never saw women hate or seem to hate one another's company more than the Roman ladies do, for in their *conversazioni* you'll see no other but the mistress of the house. These are the only evening amusements that are in Rome, as except in the Carnival there are no theatres open. Amongst the women of quality [there are] very few handsome ones; but the citizens are very handsome.
>
> The English will be all gone by next week excepting Lord Robert Spencer,** who stays here some time longer. In my next letter I will send you a *petite detaile* of what my intentions are; if they prove according to your desires I shall then be very happy.
>
> Don't you pity the Roman ladies not being able to bear any sweet smells? They can't so much as suffer flowers of any kind, though they have charming ones. Whenever I go into their villas I must own I envy them their fine orange trees out of doors. I had this morning a basket of strawberries for my breakfast. I wish I could have sent them to you, but I believe they may have them as soon in Dublin. In my opinion they have not the flavour of our strawberries.
>
> I yesterday saw a servant who left Ste Fox and Lady Mary at Marseilles in good health. Before this arrives to you I fancy they'll be in England. Our weather is very changeable and rainy. I am afraid I shall want money soon for to pay for my utensils I mentioned in my last. You'll be so kind as to make my excuses to Emily for not answering her, but writing to you is all I can find time for this post, and that hardly.

---

* The Duchess of Leinster's eyes being bad, she often employed her eldest daughter, Emily, to write letters for her.
** Son of Charles Spencer, 3rd Duke of Marlborough.

William was finding Rome nothing like Naples for gaiety. The Pope had, indeed, 'forbid all kinds of amusement'. William himself was behaving with more propriety than some of the young noblemen who made the Grand Tour; and on 9 May he wrote to his mother: 'You still make me more happy with the thoughts of your being content with my conduct'. But he added: 'I think Rome rather a dull place', admitting, however, that he had 'not yet seen everything that is to be seen here'. He was looking forward to visiting Florence before settling at Turin; but, 'I am afraid', he continued, 'that scheme will not answer as there is an epidemical disorder in Tuscany and God knows how long it may last'.

The weather had been terrible. It was now improving, but William was not happy about the great heats that he believed would soon begin. He dreaded intense heat. He continued to pass the time at the grand private assemblies – apart from sightseeing, there was nothing else to do. And in his letter to the Duchess, of 9 May, he described one of these:

> I finished Emily's letter very abruptly by saying I was in a hurry to go to a *conversazione*. I am sure the description of the mistress of the house will entertain you: she is less than Lady M-e, she has a hump back that is higher than her head, they say blind of an eye. So I won't be scandalous, but to tell the truth I did not perceive it. She is the wrong side of 60, as they say. She has about 20,000 pound sterling. I intended to have made proposals that night (though she is a double widow); but on enquiring I find her estate was not in her power, as the King of Naples is her heir.
>
> I suppose by this time Lord and Lady Holland are arrived. I expect Charles Fox here soon. Lord Robert Spencer and I are almost the only English that are here; he is an agreeable young man, as much as I have seen of him. I see by today's English newspapers that Lord Barrimore is at last married. The house that I live in is agreeably situated for walking in a charming villa that is just above me, so that I just step up and walk in my full dress and hat under the ... [word indecipherable]. I shall enjoy more when the hot weather begins, as the walks are very shady. ... P.S. I drew for money this day to clear off those articles that I mentioned in a former letter.

For William the time was now passing rapidly. He had seen everything in Rome worth seeing, and was anxious to push on to Florence. Towards the end of the month he wrote:

May the 27th, 1767 ... The house that I live in here is very well situated, for one part of it is in a manner in the country, and the other in town. The weather is as yet very pleasant, not too hot. I have now in my rooms seven of the finest carnations I ever saw. There are prodigious fine ones here. If in case you or Lady Louis should choose any of them, I know a person here that can get them best, and send them carefully to Ireland.

I must now mention a scheme of mine which, if agreeable to you and the Duke, will be a very agreeable one to me. I'll begin by mentioning that I am losing my time here, as I have seen everything there is to be seen here, and I must own Rome is a very dull place. So I propose setting out for Florence the beginning of next month. My present intentions is to stay some time; from thence to go to Pisa, Leghorn and Genoa; and then to be at Turin by the beginning of November. By making the above mentioned tour I shall have seen that part of Italy, and delay Milan, Venice, etc., etc., for after Turin; and at Turin I shall make a long stay. If I do not get away soon the weather will be too hot to travel; and there is between this and Florence places where the air is bad. I hope the Duke has no objection, but I believe I shall go to Florence with Lord Robert Spencer and Mr More, as their intentions are to go rather a roundabout way to see the waterfall of Terni, which by all accounts is very fine and worth seeing.

The month of May drew to a close, and William was still in Rome. His time was, as usual, fully occupied. He was now buying things which in later years would remind him of his visit such as books and engravings. This was the period during which Piranesi was working in Rome, and his engravings had achieved immense popularity. Piranesi had already published many plates. He worked with astonishing speed; before starting on a subject he would observe it by day and by night in order to grasp the best effects of light and shade and the most dramatic angle of perspective. In his search for new subjects he would wander through the Roman countryside, hacking his way through the dense vegetation with a hatchet and lighting fires to frighten away scorpions. He was employed in repairing and restoring churches by William's friend, the Pope; who knighted him, warning him that his knight's sword should only be used to defend the Roman Faith. Piranesi had a violent temper; he had already twice attempted murder.

Besides making hurried last-minute purchases, William was going round saying goodbye to all his friends. In the midst of his bustling activity he rushed to his writing table, took up his quill pen and pulled out some paper:

> June the 3rd, 1767 ... whenever I have a few minutes to spare I cannot pass them better than in writing a few lines to you. I propose setting out either Saturday or Sunday for Florence. I hope you approve of the schemes I sent you in my last of the 27th of last month. I hope the Duke will not take it amiss, but I shall have a box to send to Ireland, of some prints and books of antiquities which would take rather too much place for to carry about with me. There are the prints of some of the most famous pictures at Rome. I bind them so that they pay no more duty that if it was one. So I hope if there is any particular ones that you or Lady Louisa like, I hope you'll take them. And there are some things that will be worth your while looking over, and I dare say amuse you ... I hope you'll excuse this short letter, as I am a going to make my last visits.

Three days later, on the eve of his departure, William was in a flurry of preparations for his journey. No doubt Mr Bolle was busy packing his fine clothes, and organising arrangements for the carriage, and for the footmen that invariably accompanied a noble Lord.

> June the 6th, 1767. In the midst of my hurry, I just have a minute to embrace the opportunity of writing to you; though I should have had more pleasure if I had a letter to answer, as the last date I received is the 30th April. The weather seems to promise for heat for our journey. There was on Thursday night last a pretty violent earthquake here. It is imagined that it has done some mischief somewhere in the country, but unluckily for me I slept so well that I did not feel it. I hope you'll excuse the shortness of this letter, as I leave this tomorrow, and nothing new to say but that I am eat up with fleas ... P.S. I have drawn for money.

And so William and his tutor climbed into the carriage, and rumbled through the muddy streets and out into the flat Roman countryside. With him William took inescapable memories of the ancient city; the noble families – the Giustinianis and Countess Mahony; his friend, the Pope – that upright, pacific old man whose pontificate was so unquiet; the palaces with their magnificent collections of pictures and statues; the baroque churches; the mobile carving of the Bernini fountains; the Piazza di Spagna, where the ladies sat at their ease in their coaches receiving the homage of the gentlemen who stood at their coach doors; swarming beggars, innumerable monks – that strange population of which it had been said a quarter were priests, a quarter statues and a quarter people did nothing; the sluggish yellow water of the Tiber; the Piazza Navona with its Bernini fountain and Borromini church; the evening parade of fine carriages up and down the Corso; the cattle wandering down the Sacred Way to the market in the Forum; the dull red brick of the Coliseum stripped of its marble; the shaft of sunlight bursting through the top of the Pantheon; the forbidding castle of St Angelo; the dome of St Peter's receding with every step until it became a tiny cupola only a fraction larger than those of the other churches all dominating the huddle of roofs; and the grand and melancholy arches of the broken aqueducts that stalked the silent countryside.

4

FLORENCE

Every visitor to Florence entered the famous capital of the Italian Renaissance with a sense of wonder and excitement. But William had an added and very special reason for interest. It was from Florence 800 years previously that his Italian ancestors, the Gherardini, had set out northward through France and England to the conquest of Ireland. The main branch of the family had continued to reside there right through the Middle Ages. Arriving in Florence was for William something in the nature of a homecoming.

William spent six days on the road from Rome. The journey is best described in his own words:

> Florence, June the 14th, 1767. My dearest Mother, I arrived here the night before last, having made a most agreeable journey through the most beautiful country I ever saw. We did not come the straight road from Rome, but went across country to see a prodigious fine waterfall, at a place called Terni. There falls more water than at Powerscourt, but I do not think so high, nor just where the water falls is not quite so beautiful. But the ride to it is most delightful. To give you a description of the whole country I passed through would be doing it injustice, as it is impossible for anybody to describe the real beauties with justice, nor without seeing of them can one hardly believe it. There is wood, water and everything that can add to make a country beautiful.

And so William came to the little conical hills and the cypresses that surround Florence. Over the hills to his left was the country of the Val d'Elsa, where the original Gherardini had had their estates: a fertile country of woods and vineyards, and hills crowned with little castles. Away to his right lay Vallombrosa. The valley of the Arno brought William to his first view of the Renaissance city. On either side of him stretched groves of dusty green olive trees, interspersed here and there with bright red mulberries. Below him, serene and eternal, enfolded within the wooded encircling hills, lay the colourful mass of stone and marble. Above the tiled roofs rose the exquisite warm red curves of Brunelleschi's cupola, Giotto's black and white campanile, and the graceful tower of the Palazzo Vecchio. The clear light of a June evening, with the sun setting in a fiery sky straight ahead of him, silhouetting the towers and pinnacles, and illuminating every facet of every building with a wonderful sharpness, gave William perhaps the most perfect first impression of the city that he could possibly have wished for. As the light grew less, and darkness began to blur the outlines of the landscape, he would see the fireflies darting among the olive leaves, he would hear one by one the cigalas begin their nocturnal song, when the air would be filled with their continuous chirping. Soon only the cypresses would be distinguishable, standing like jet needles against the dark sky. But the country, with its smells and sounds peculiar to a June night, William now left behind, as his carriage rumbled over the Arno and plunged into the narrow Florentine streets.

William settled into the social life very quickly. His letter of 14 June states:

> Florence seems to be an agreeable place enough. The people are very much inclined to be civil to the English. Then I had letters to some of the first people here. One was for Comte Rosanbergh, who is the Prime Minister here, who says he knew you and the Duke in England. He is a German and was in England four years, and is very fond of the English. I enquired of the Cardinal Corrini at Rome, who knows the origin of our family and says it is Geraldini, and he told me that there was none of that name left. But I shall certainly know if there is. I have not yet been presented at Court, as I have no proper mourning till today. I am now in the country for to complete myself in my Italian, so I hope to stay some time. I have the same master as Mr Connolly had when he was here. Pray, ask him if he knows the Abbé Pilloni. The post goes out at 12 o'clock, and it is now near it, so I must conclude in assuring you I am ever your most affectionate son, KILDARE. My love to the Duke, etc., etc., at Carton, Blackrock, Dublin. I am very much afraid I shall want a little money by the next post.

The Cardinal Corrini mentioned by William was probably Cardinal Nerio Maria Corsini, a member of a Florentine princely family whose palace overlooks the River Arno, and nephew of a former pope, Clement XII. He was now 82 years old, and was to live another three years.

The Tuscan Court was in mourning for Josepha, second wife of the Emperor Joseph II, whose brother ruled Tuscany as Grand Duke Leopold I and later succeeded him on the imperial throne as Leopold II. They were both sons of the Empress Maria Theresa and the Emperor Francis I. Leopold had succeeded to the Grand Duchy on the death of his father two years earlier. His wife was Maria Louisa, daughter of Charles III of Spain and sister of Ferdinand King of Naples. At this time the Grand Duke was twenty years of age. He became a very great ruler; and under his enlightened government Tuscany was transformed into the most progressive state in all Italy.

Having obtained his mourning clothes, William was ready to be presented at Court. He did not have long to wait.

> Saturday, June the 20th, 1767 ... Since my last I have had the honour of being presented to the Grand Duke and Duchess, who seem to be a very amiable young couple. I am to dine with them on Monday. He is very much liked here. You will certainly like him for his good nature. When he heard his Mother was so ill of the smallpox, he wanted to set out post to Vienna for to see her. The loss of the young Empress does not seem to affect any of them here, and, by what I hear, her death is full as little regretted at Vienna, though they all say she was good-natured but terribly ugly.

The Emperor Joseph had been devoted to his first wife, Isabella, daughter of Philip, Duke of Parma, and never recovered emotionally from her death in 1763. His second wife he married for dynastic reasons. He did not love her; and her death this year (1767) left him unmoved. He refused to marry a third time.

The Grand Duke Leopold's mother, the empress Maria Theresa, was at this time also ill with smallpox, and great anxiety was felt at the Tuscan Court on her account.

> This seems to be an agreeable place enough, though I must own I am very much disappointed, as I expected to have found it a more beautiful place.
>
> It is astonishing the number of ugly women there are in this town. And there is but one or two handsome women of fashion in the town; one of which is a Roman lady married here. I can't find anything very enchanting either in their person or their conversation to have conquered the hearts of so many English. I dare say you have heard of Lord Cooper, who has been here these eight years. He is

quite a *cavaliere servante* or *Cicisbée* to a lady here who is far from handsome: he attends her regularly wherever she goes, gives her the arm, keeps her pocket handkerchief, takes care of her cloak, when she goes into company, goes her messages. But they are beginning to grow tired of one another.

George Nassau Clavering-Cowper had succeeded his father as third Earl of Cowper three years earlier. He was at this time 29 years old. Later he was created by Joseph II a Prince of the Holy Roman Empire. It is said that the girl he married was instrumental in getting this title for him, she being a favourite of the Emperor's brother, Leopold, Grand Duke of Tuscany. Lord Cowper had a villa near Florence.

It was the fashion for a man to choose a married woman, attend upon her daily, and become her *cicisbeo*. He accompanied her to parties, where she was seldom seen with her husband. Lady Holland, who, as we have already seen, had passed through Florence on her homeward journey the previous April, had seen enough of Italian social life to make her sound a note of warning to William's mother in a letter from Turin: 'I think him[*] as safe as most young men, as I don't think him apt to be in love. But, dear sister, don't leave him too long in Italy; except virtu, nothing is to be learnt in it. The women are dangerous in every respect, nothing to be learnt from them, vice and illness frequently got by them and if once a young man becomes a real *cicisbeo* 'tis a lounging idle life which when once got into is difficult to get out of. There is Lord Cooper has been eight years now abroad, and has not the heart to go home. I do assure you I should have great uneasiness at leaving Charles, but that he won't be long in any of the places, and that I think his love of politics and desire of making a figure at home will always call him back; besides, I don't see any disposition towards the ladies of Italy in him ... what makes me afraid is seeing Mr Upton at his time of life so very ridiculously in love with an impudent looking woman at Naples, as to propose returning in the summer again to Italy. My advice would be to let William run thro' Italy, see what's to be seen, then as he is military and that his father likes he should be so, send him to Germany. Vienna is much commended by many people. I have given you my thoughts, sweet Siss. I may judge wrong, but it is my real opinion.'

I dare say Lady Holland in her letters mentioned Sir Horace Mann, our

[*] William.

Minister here. He is the greatest old woman I ever met with; but, give him his due, he is very civil.

Sir Horace Mann, now 66 years old, had already spent 27 years as British Minister at the Court of Tuscany; he was to retain the appointment until his death nineteen years later. His post was an important one; indeed, the English Resident at Florence was more influential than all the other English diplomatists in the rest of Italy put together, for he had to protect the interests of the English mercantile colony at Leghorn. And Leghorn was the most important trading port on the coast. Like William Hamilton at Naples, Mann counted it a large part of his duty to entertain English visitors, and to introduce them into Italian society. He lived in the Casa Mannetti, by the Ponte de Trinita. It was in this house, soon after his first arrival, that he entertained another young man – Horace Walpole. But 27 years of court life had left their mark: and it is hardly to be wondered at that William found the Minister 'the greatest old woman I ever met with'. Mann himself, shortly afterwards, spoke with contempt of the insipidity and dull weariness of the *conversazioni* which he had both to attend and to give.

> There is to be great doings here for the latter end of summer for the Queen of Naples, who stops here on her way to Naples. It is said that the Emperor has some thoughts of coming with her, but it is not yet certain.

The Queen of Naples, for whom there were to be 'great doings' towards the end of the summer, was the luckless Maria Josepha, a daughter of the Empress Maria Theresa, and sister of the Grand Duke Leopold of Tuscany and the Emperor Joseph. She married Ferdinand, King of Naples, by proxy in August of this year, but died on the day appointed for her journey to Italy. Maria Theresa, however, had plenty of daughters; another, Maria Carolina was despatched the following year to Ferdinand and became his wife.

> We have a chariot and a horse race next week, which will be curious, as it is something in the antique way.

These chariot and horse races were undoubtedly those held in the Piazza Santa Maria Novella. Here, overlooked by Albert's black and white marble façade at the one end, and, at the other, by

Brunelleschi's Loggia and della Robbia's terracotta medallions, were run the Roman Chariot Races. Started in 1563 by Cosimo I, they were held under the grand Dukes every Midsummer Eve. The two obelisks, which rest on tortoises, were the goal posts.

The weather was now delightfully warm. Like Horace Walpole many years before, William dressed himself in a nightgown. He wrote:

> June 27th, 1767 ... I may now really say the weather is hot. Till within these few days it has been very pleasant, but now it'll be more so. There is no going out from 10 in the morning till 7 at night. I am now in a light lustring night-gown, though at the same time I am as hot as Jack FitzPatrick ever was in the kitchen. The only way of keeping oneself tolerably cool is to keep the windows and window shutters shut, by way of keeping out the sun.
>
> Bolle writ to Lady Cecilia last post to let you know I had not time to write as I dined with the Grand Duke, who really gave us a very excellent dinner. He is a civil, well-bred, amiable young man, a great deal to say for himself, and has had a very good education. He is beloved by everybody here. At dinner Sir Horace Mann sat next to him and I next to the Grand Duchess, who is also very amiable, but not handsome. She talked a great deal at dinner. They seem to be very fond of one another. They are both very fond of the Empress-Queen, who is now entirely recovered. She would have been a great loss to this country, as well as to her own. It is strongly reported that the Emperor will be here in September with his sister, the Queen of Naples, who stays here some time before she goes to Naples. So there'll be great feasts here, such as masquerade, balls, operas, etc., etc. I hope the Duke will have no objection to my being here; then as I propose either going to Pisa or Lucca for a month or so as there are baths and waters that are very good for me, then to turn back again to Florence, as it is an agreeable town, and then if the Emperor comes there'll be magnificent doings. But anyhow I'll be at Turin in November and stay as long as you please.

To dine with the Grand Duke at the Pitti Palace, his official residence, must have been an impressive experience. We may well imagine William driving over the Ponte Vecchio, along the narrow Via Guicciardini and into the wide cobbled space before the palace. Up the slope in front of the vast façade the carriage rattled and entered the gateway into the covered courtyard. The carriage stopped, William alighted, and, preceded by gold-laced footmen, proceeded up the long flights of magnificent stone stairs until he reached the great gallery. Here he entered the decorated rooms with their rich ceilings – the walls hung with the paintings of the first Italian masters – and was received by the Grand Duke and his Duchess. After dinner, when he sat next to the Grand Duchess, he and his hosts and Sir Horace Mann and the other guests no doubt walked in the exquisite Boboli gardens. Up the steps which climb the steep hill, among the statues and the high clipped hedges, wandered the ladies in their rustling taffeta dresses, the gentlemen in their no-less gaudy silks and velvets whispering words of endearment which were lost in the murmur of fountains, or speaking of European affairs, or of the Imperial family. Below them, the dusky panorama of the city with its moonlit domes and towers; and the slumbering hills, their forms visible through the dark cypress trees that stood, tall and sentinel, amidst the groves and statuary of the Pitti Palace gardens.

> I am rather sorry I was not at Venice this year as everybody says the fête was the most magnificent that ever was seen. It was all for the Duke of Wittembergh [Wurttemberg], who is one of the most curious men that ever was heard of. His Court allows him a pension to live out of his state. He has taken 3 *pallazes* at Venice and 4 country houses. He has quite turned the Venetian heads. He took a great deal of notice of the English; he gave 2 or 3 balls on purpose for them.
>
> I was at a horse race and a chariot race here; it is very curious as the horses have no riders. I was on the same balcony as the Grand Duke was, who was very civil to Lord Robert Spencer and I; he made us come and stand by him, by which means we got a good place.

July came. William had now been abroad just a year, and he and his tutor were taking financial stock:

> July the 4th, 1767 ... Bolle has writ to the Duke this post, wherein he mentions the money spent and received this last quarter. It is this very day year that we left London. I am really ashamed when I consider the money I have spent, during this year. But it shall be my best endeavours, to make this next year less expensive, as the first year there was a great many things wanting which will not this year. I can assure you nothing makes me happier than when I imagine that you and my father are pleased with my conduct, which I flatter myself you are, by the many kindnesses I have received from you. I am afraid there is one article in Bolle's quarterly account that is unreasonable, which is my pocket money; but that was while I was Rome, I lost some money at

loo with the Countess of Mahony, for I never won, and it run rather high.

William had just heard from Charles Fox, who told him he proposed staying in Italy some time, and was hoping to come to Florence soon with Lord Fitzwilliam. Letters from home, however, had not arrived for some time; but William imagined they had gone to Rome, from which place the post arrived only once a week. The weather was now hotter than ever; William found the heat 'almost insupportable':

> July 11th, 1767 ... Our weather is terribly hot, and poor William will be as thin as a whipping post before it is long, as he loses his appetite and does not sleep and sw--ts like a horse that has run a race. For the heat is insupportable, and he can't eat ices for they give him the gripes, which you know he is subject to. I think the poor boy is very much to be pity'd, and all the comfort he has from Sir Horace Mann is that [it is a] common complaint in summer.
>
> Sir Horace is to have a magnificent *conversazione* tonight in his garden, which is to be illuminated; it'll be very agreeable, as at present there are but few amusements at Florence.
>
> I believe I never mentioned the lady Sir Horace is *Cicisbée* to. He is very convenient to her, as she loves good eating and drinking, which she makes Sir Horace give her whenever she chooses. She does nothing but talk of it, and is always enquiring when the water melons come in, as she may eat them, she says, till she swells, which is her comfort.
>
> I cannot say the Florentines are the most agreeable people or the easiest got acquainted with of any in Italy. The men are better looking set of people; in general, the ladies are horridly ugly; it is not to be told how uncommon a thing a handsome woman is here.

William was still expecting the Emperor to visit the city. Meanwhile, he continued to amuse himself in fashionable society. Although the July days were stiflingly hot, he found it possible to get out and take the air in the evenings:

> 18th of July, 1767 ... Our weather still continues very hot, but by use not so disagreeable as it was at first; the evenings are very pleasant, as there generally is a little air, and falls little or no dew ... I, thank God, pass my time as agreeably as possible ... The Emperor comes here with the Queen of Naples upon a visit to his brother. They say he proposes making a tour of Europe, and means to go to England. He is to stop at Turin to see whether one of the Duchesses of Savoy will suit him for a

wife. He is an unlucky man to have buried two wives at five and twenty years old.

The amusements are not very numerous in this town. The fashionable one is walking upon the bridge at night, and in the evening they go and sit in their coaches the outside of one of the gates of the town. They say it is by way of getting fresh air. I believe it is to pick up all the waste dust that is flying about, as it is upon the Bologna road, and there pass a great many carriages of all sorts. It is the fashion here for men to carry fans; you know I like to be in the fashion, so I have got myself one, and when I dine at home I make use of it; and I also take it to bed and fan myself to sleep, which is very comfortable in this oven. But one meets the friars and all the gentlemen with them walking the streets of an evening.

June 21st, 1767. My dearest Mother, I had yesterday the pleasure of receiving Emily's letter of the 24th of June, which made me very happy in finding a postscript of your own handwriting. I certainly shall be very willing to do anything that'll be of service to my health and a satisfaction to you. At present I find myself perfectly well, but intend taking the sea the latter end of August. At present the weather is too hot for to undertake any journey. The only thing to be done now is to keep oneself as cool as possible. Yesterday and the day before were the hottest days we have had yet. I heard a person say that they were the hottest days that he ever felt in Italy. If these 2 days past had come about a fortnight ago that they would have killed, but now I am used to it, it is not so disagreeable, but bad enough.

I shall write for your carnations on Saturday; I hope they'll answer. If Jacob Smith will have them packed up in any particular way, you'll let me know. I do not think you can get them till October.*

It has already been remarked that William had now been abroad just over a year. He was eighteen years and four months old, and the question of a possible marriage for him was in the air. Lady Catherine Annesley being already married, another young Lady now comes on the scene. Oddly enough, her name is Miss FitzGerald:

I do not [continued William on July 21st] dislike Emily's description of Miss FitzGerald. I should have been glad to have seen her; pray, how old is she?

* It has already been said that when William was in Rome he greatly admired the fine carnations, and asked his mother whether she would like him to send her some. She had evidently replied asking him to do so. It would be interesting to know whether those growing at Carton until recently were from this stock.

William's sister, Emily, had evidently written to him, no doubt at her mother's request, about the young lady, telling him that she was a suitable person to whom he might become engaged. This, of course, was not unusual at a time when *marriages de convenance* were arranged by the parents of the young people concerned. But it was natural, to say the least, that William should have expressed a desire to see his future wife before the engagement, and to be informed of her age. As regards the material aspect of the match, things could hardly have been improved upon: Caroline, daughter of Richard FitzGerald Esq., of Mount Ophaly in County Kildare, was heiress of the Mitchelstown estates, then worth £6,000 a year, besides large personal property.

William was far more studious than most young men who made the Grand Tour. Few bothered to learn even the rudiments of Italian or French; and in society preferred to mix with their own compatriots. There were, of course, exceptions; notably William's brilliant young cousin, Charles Fox, who thoroughly mastered both languages; and their friend and contemporary, Lord Carlisle. 'I go on very well with my Italian,' went on William on 21 July:

> I am now reading poetry, which is very pretty. I have a very good master; to be sure, it is a charming language. I expect Charles Fox every day. Lord Robert Spencer leaves this next week. Lord FitzWilliam is also expected. It is amazing wherever one goes the number of English one meets. There are a dozen here at present; they all seem inclined to stay. My chief amusement here of an evening is to go to a most beautiful meadow which looks quite English, which is surrounded by trees and the river runs just by it. It is a delightful place for to cool oneself after the heat of the day.

Apart from that of his cousin and immediate friends, William preferred the society of Italians. This, together with his seriousness and nice manners, must have made him stand a good deal higher in Sir Horace Mann's opinion than the average young English boy who came to Florence with his tutor. Walpole had a very poor view of these young gentlemen and their governors – especially the latter, whom he called 'boobies' – and in his letters to Mann commiserated with him on having to entertain them. Neither had Lady Holland any high idea of the Englishmen she met in Italy.

At home William's father, the Duke of Leinster, was not neglecting his son's army future. In those days commissions were bought, and the officer's presence with his regiment seemed unnecessary. On 1 August William wrote to his mother:

> to thank the Duke for his obliging remembrance of me in purchasing the lieutenancy. I hope he means to do just as he pleases about my remaining or advancing in the army, as I am sure whatever pleases him is agreeable to me, as I shall do and have done everything in my power to oblige him. I can assure you that it makes me very happy to think he has been so well pleased with my conduct since I have left you.

It will be recalled that when William was sixteen he had received a commission, as cornet, in General Honeywood's troop of horse.

William was hoping, about the middle of this month (August), to make a tour to Lucca, Pisa, and then to Leghorn, where he would bathe in the sea. He was supporting the heat better than he had done; the night of 31 July had brought rain, which had cooled the air a little. He missed the good Irish fruit; the local fruit he found 'hardly eatable'. The figs were very good, the peaches very bad. The water melons he had not yet tasted; but they did look good. There were no pineapples. The English had almost all gone, but a new set had arrived, among them Lord FitzWilliam. Charles Fox had gone to Turin to meet Lord Carlisle, who, William imagined, had no thoughts of coming.

Lord FitzWilliam was a year older than William. He had been at Eton with William, Charles Fox and Lord Carlisle, and his portrait still hangs, with those of Fox and Carlisle, in the Provost's Lodge. Later he became Lord Lieutenant of Ireland, where his popularity was such that when he left, the people of Dublin shut their shops, and are said to have gone into mourning.

> I am afraid the Emperor will not be here before November. His chief reason for making this journey is to have an opportunity of seeing the sea and ships. It sounds odd for a person to come so many hundred miles for to see the sea when there are many that had rather go some hundred miles than [see the] sea and the ships.

The Emperor's Tuscan navy, consisting of a few frigates, was commanded by an Englishman called Acton. He had been an East India Company captain, and was uncle of Sir John Acton of Neapolitan fame.

'I could wish,' added William, perhaps a little sadly, 'the Florentines were easier to get acquainted with.'

His expenses still continued high. He again drew for a hundred pounds. But he had made a new rule of paying everything immediately.

William was now about halfway through his stay in Florence. His future plans occupied his mind a good deal: he had thoughts of ending his Grand Tour with a visit to Barèges, a watering place first made fashionable by Madame de Maintenon's visit in 1677.

August the 8th, 1767. I am very sorry to be obliged to begin my letter by saying that it is time to finish, as the post is just going out. I was yesterday in the country and did not return till 4 o'clock this morning, and got up too late, as the post goes out at eleven. It was very pleasant in he country, as the weather is not so hot, as we have had a good deal of rain, which has cooled the air very much.

Charles Fox is at last come and gives us a very good account of Lord Holland. The last letter from home was dated the 2nd of July. I hope you received mine of the 1st of this month. I hear Lady Holland has wrote to you about my going to Barèges; but, thank God, I continue very well and propose taking the sea bathing this month. My love to the Duke, etc., etc. I am, my dearest Mother, ever your most affectionate son, KILDARE.

5

FLORENCE – LEGHORN – LUCCA – FLORENCE

'I am very sorry,' wrote William on August 11th, 'to hear the Duke of York has some thoughts of spending the winter at Turin; I shall be ashamed of him, especially if he does not behave better than he did last time he was abroad; wherever he has been they complain of him. I do not know how they'll receive him if he goes to Rome, as they are very angry with him, and not without reason. Anyhow he'll not do very well after Prince of Brunswick, who is so much liked in Italy (*il est un Prince digne, et l'autre n'est pas digne d'estre Prince*).

Prince Edward Augustus, second son of Frederick, Prince of Wales, was 28 years old. On the accession to the throne of his brother as George III, he had been created Duke of York. He was a dissolute man, and amorous. But he appears to have been singularly unattractive to girls. William's aunt, Lady Sarah Lennox, called him 'that ugly little white pig'. His reputation abroad was bad; everywhere he had been people had been talking about him; and William did not relish the thought of spending the winter with him at Turin. But William need not have worried: within six weeks the Duke was dead.

Meanwhile, the social life in Florence was improving:

Florence is rather more agreeable than it was, as people begin to have small parties; though, to be sure, to me they are not quite so pleasant as a large *conversazione*, as here there is no loo playing, and as for other games I know none. Though I mentioned loo I would always rather not play, as cards are my aversion.

The Grand Duke and Duchess were yesterday evening at Marquis Riccardi's to see a horse race.* The *palazzo* is magnificent and largest and richest furnished I have ever seen. We had a concert of musick, and ices brought about; there was a great many people and the house was illuminated and all the rooms open, which had a very good effect.

* Racing with riderless horses was customary in the main streets of Italian cities.

Florence will be very gay when the Emperor and Queen of Naples come.

What a wonderful experience it must have been to visit the Riccardi palace – and on a festive occasion – while it was still lived in! The Riccardi family acquired the palace in the seventeenth century; but it will always be associated with the previous owners – the Medici. Like the Strozzi palace, it is built of rusticated stone, supporting a splendid projecting roof, a feature typical of Florence. We can imagine on that summer evening the flaring torches placed at regular intervals in the iron torch-holders embedded in the stonework of the walls; the rich-ly-dressed ladies and gentlemen driving into the great doorway in their carriages and being set down in the courtyard, then climbing the great stone staircase, their steps lighted by torch-bearing footmen. We can imagine William amongst the crowd, wandering through the illu-minated rooms, and under Giordano's great painted ceiling, the apotheosis of the Medici family, and perhaps in a quiet moment entering the tiny Medici chapel to feast his eyes upon Gozzoli's cav-alcade where the fresh, youthful face of the fifteen-year-old Lorenzo the Magnificent looks down as he rides nobly by, dressed in scarlet and gold, on his white horse; where the three charming Medici sis-ters, young and innocent, are grouped together, their long curls sur-mounted by flat round hats into which are stuck tall vertical feathers; where the Tuscan countryside is dotted with little flowers; where the mountains fill the background – a glimpse of Paradise itself in this masterpiece of colour, conception and craftsmanship. Some of the great events in Florentine history had taken place in this palace. It was here that Capponi told Charles VIII: 'Sound your trumpets and we will ring our bells'. It was from here, too, that it was proclaimed that Tuscan was no true dialect but the true language of Italy.

William kept to his self-imposed rule of writing once a week to his mother. Since his last letter, in which he had told her that the hot weather had gone, the temperature had once again risen; the very day he wrote had turned out to be the hottest he had had this year:

August the 18th, 1767 ... To be sure, the heat last week was too much for any Christian. A great many old people here say they never felt it so hot at Florence, but we have had some rain, which I now hope has cooled the air. I propose setting out very soon for Lucca and Pisa. The former is a very agreeable town and there is a theatre now open, which is no bad thing in such a small town as Lucca; and then their Italian is very good. The other is much such a place as Malvern or any water drinking place; a great deal of gaming.

I was yesterday to wait upon Count Rosanberg, but did not find him at home. The first opportunity I shall deliver him your message. I was to have dined with him last Sunday, but I was out of town. Your vases I'll bespeak this day. If I thought you was in no very great hurry I would write to Rome for some pretty antique drawings.

I wish at the same time allow you to send you a beautiful small miniature picture of a holy family which can be done for 15 guineas. I am sure you would like it. The original is by Raphael and there is a man here who copies it in miniature very well. Do let me know whether you'll have it or not.

William was a man of his time in admiring the work of Renaissance artists more than that of others; but, in suggesting a copy, he was wiser than some of his contemporaries, who were often duped into buying sham 'Raphaels' and 'Andrea del Sartos'.

I amuse myself very well here. There is a very good set of English here, six or seven old school-fellows. We expect Lord Carlisle, but God knows when; Charles Fox flatters himself with the hopes in less than a week. I have entirely got the better of everybody that have wanted me to play, though at the same time I must do my friend, Charles, the justice to say he never asked me, as he saw I did not like it. I do not see that gaming that people say there is in Italy. Rome, Naples and here all games of hazard are forbid on pain of being sent to their country. At Pisa they allow a pharaoh table during the season for the drinking the waters.

I find myself very well in regard to the humours that I had in spring; I believe the hot weather has done me good, as I have heard say that a natural perspiration was very good. I am sure if anything is the matter it is not for want of perspiration, especially last week – I slept in the Italian custom, without a shirt and nothing but a sheet. I perspired as if I was wrapped up in a flannels, and set before the kitchen fire. Pray, my love to the Duke and all the family at Black Rock, Dublin, and Carton; a few kisses to the rats ... Bolle has a kind of a rash that is natural to the country in this hot weather, he does not like. I think he looks much better than he did, and I believe is, but will not allow it.

There is an Abbé Count de Guasco that says he knew you very well in England; he talks a great deal about the late Duke of Richmond; also an Abbé Niccolini.

The 'late Duke of Richmond' was William's maternal grandfather. He too had made the Grand Tour. That was in 1719, when he was eighteen years old. Before setting out on his travels he had been married to Lady Sarah Cadogan, who was still a child and whom he considered a 'dowdy'. But three years later he returned to find her grown beyond recognition into one of the most beautiful women of her day.

The time for William's expedition to Lucca drew near; but his departure was delayed:

> August the 22nd, 1767. I intended to have set off this day for Lucca, but Tuesday next is the Grand Duchess day. It is but proper I should delay my journey a few days as it is reckoned a compliment to go to Court, and as they have always been very civil, I think it is my duty to shew a kind of regard for them. I delivered your compliments to Mon. de Rosanberg, who is *très sensible de votre bonte;* and I asked him about the Prince Lobkowitz, who, he says, is altered; instead of being gay and lively, he lives at home and sees nobody and is turned bigot.

Twenty-two years before, Prince Joseph Lobkowitz had been a giddy young visitor to London. He had become a friend of William's mother, who was then the beautiful young Lady Emily Lennox. Gorgeously dressed, he had walked under the trees in Vauxhall Gardens, and played practical jokes on the Venetian Ambassadress. And now the wheel of time had turned the good-natured, wild young man into a recluse.

William continued his letter of 22 August:

> I have bespoke your vases; I hope you'll like them. The small ones I may venture to say will please you, they are quite different patterns and also different shapes. The large pair I have not yet determined on, but he is altering the drawing of it. They will not be done sooner than 3 months. When they are finished, would you have them sent immediately, or stay till spring?
>
> I hear Lord Holland is to be at Nice this winter. Do you mean that I should spend the winter with them? If you do, you'll alter the schemes of Turin. I shall have no objection if you have none, of going and making them a visit, as it is, I believe, but a few days' journey.

William was enjoying having his cousin with him; together with Lord FitzWilliam they went to parties given by the Florentine nobility.

Charles Fox has persuaded himself that he is in love, and I believe he means to enter into *Cicibéeship*. But the misfortune of Charles is that he is apt to be very neglectful of her and not see the lady for 2 days, then he is obliged to begin again. The lady seems to have not objection to him, but I believe between you and I Lord FitzWilliam is the one she has fixed her eye upon.

Charles Fox's time was at present much occupied with learning Italian, of which he was 'immoderately fond'. He read nothing else. He loved especially the Italian poetry. Writing to Lady Mary Fox's brother, Richard FitzPatrick – who was *en pension* at Caen, where he learnt French and attended the Military Academy – he said, 'For God's sake learn Italian as fast as you can, if it be only to read Ariosto. There is more good poetry in Italian than in all other languages that I understand put together. In prose too it is a very fine language'.

'I am going to a concert this morning,' concluded William on 22 August, 'to hear a most famous singer. I am grown quite a lover of musick.'

William was now able to spend a few days away from Florence; it was, therefore, a little over a week before he wrote again – this time from Leghorn:

Leghorn, September the 4th, 1767. My dearest Mother, I have been rather neglectful this last post or two but have constantly hurry by travelling. I could get no other place than Leghorn for to bathe in the sea. I have been in three times and it agrees with me very well. I do think Italy the prettiest country I ever saw; the variety of scenes that one sees is delightful. I stopped at Lucca, which is a pretty town. I mean, when I return to Florence, to stop there and at Pisa.

The little city of Lucca was popular with tourists. The Italian spoken there was very pure, living was cheap. Besides its fine architecture and paintings, it had a beautiful promenade round the ramparts, and the surrounding country was charming. Foreigners were invariably welcomed with an evening serenade. It was evidently an orderly city, for pistols and swords had to be given up at the gate of entry, and were returned when the tourist departed.

William continued his letter from Leghorn:

This is not a pretty or a large town, but the number of people one sees in the streets is astonishing. But what pleases me is to see the number of different nations gather together; they speak all languages. There is at present one of our men-of-war, and a frigate; I am going this day to dine aboard. The Governor of the town is a very good sort of a man, I have dined with him twice.

Leghorn was the most important port on the west coast of Italy. Its prosperity began when it was bought by the Florentines in 1421. At the beginning of the seventeenth century the port and harbour were opened to traders of all nationalities, and since 1691 it had been a free port. The great increase in the population which took place during the eighteenth century was at the expense mainly of Pisa – which now had the appearance of a deserted city – and, to a certain extent, of Florence. A flourishing trade was carried on with England. Already in 1730 36 English families resided there. By now the city contained many English merchants, who were regarded with respect. Indeed, among the foreign merchants, the English held the chief place, the Dutch being their main competitors. English trading ships were continually coming in and out of the harbour. Owing to the constant communication with England, English travellers found it convenient to use Leghorn as a port of entry or departure. And they were pleased on arrival to discover so many of the inhabitants able to converse with them in fairly good English. Although Leghorn was essentially a commercial town, there were some interesting buildings, among which was the seventeenth-century cathedral, with its façade designed by Inigo Jones.

The presence of English warships in the harbour is a reminder of the necessity for the provision of adequate protection in the Mediterranean for merchant ships against Barbary pirates. Regular tribute was paid to these robbers by the great European powers to insure the safety of their vessels. The rulers of the Italian states were too weak to get rid of these buccaneers. Italian merchantmen when at sea flew the flag of another country in order to safeguard themselves from attack and probable capture.

William's being invited to dinner onboard an English naval ship, and by the Governor of Leghorn, and generally enjoying the society of the most intelligent and interesting men wherever he stayed, must have pleased his parents. For it was true that many travellers saw only the outsides of things, 'monuments rather than men, inns rather than houses, routes rather than the country'.

Once more William heard news of the unpopular Duke of York:

The Duke of York, we hear, is at Genoa, which I am very sorry for, as I am afraid he'll come into this part of the world, and he'll be very troublesome, as they really hate him wherever he has been; his behaviour all over Italy has been abominable; I hope he means to retrieve his lost character.

William spent the greater part of September at Leghorn. He found the bathing there excellent:

Leghorn, September the 17th, 1767. I have been very regular in my bathing since I have been here, and find it agrees with me very well, and hope it'll be in my power to reap the advantage of bathing somewhere or other next spring, either at Genoa or Venice. I hope you mean that I should stay in Italy another year and then to go home, and take Germany in the second expedition. As Germany is a country that I should like to see very well, I am sorry the Emperor has retarded his journey till November, as that has broke into some of my schemes. This is not the most agreeable town in the world, but, to be sure, worth seeing; everybody seems occupied.

Throughout his travels William sustained his interest in affairs at home in Ireland:

I am sorry that Lord Townsend is our Lord Lieutenant, as I fear [it] is not agreeable for some friends of ours, especially as he is, by all accounts, a strange man and not to be depended upon.

George Townshend, 4th Viscount Townshend – who had succeeded his father in the title in 1764, and who had taken chief command at Quebec on Wolfe's death in 1759 – had been appointed Lord Lieutenant of Ireland the previous month. He was to retain the post until September 1772. During his five years Viceroyalty he did more to corrupt and lower political life in Ireland than any previous Lord Lieutenant. 'Lord Townshend,' wrote Lecky, the historian, 'is one of the very small number of Irish Viceroys who have been personally disliked.'

The Duke of York (continued William) is expected every day at Genoa; from thence he comes to Florence ... I shall be obliged to make a fine coat or 2 for the arrival of the Queen of Naples, as we are to have great doings at Florence. The last money we drew for here we got a great deal more for a hundred pound than at Florence or Rome, etc., etc.; for which reason I hope the Duke will have no objection to my drawing again here, as I shall have my clothes to pay for. It'll be more advantageous to me.

William now said goodbye to his friends at Leghorn, and started on his journey back to Florence. As he had planned, he made a stop at Lucca on the way:

Lucca, September 25th, 1767. My dearest Mother, I am much obliged to you for your obliging letter of the 21st of August, which, I can assure you, makes me very happy when I think the Duke is pleased with my conduct; in regard to money, you may be sure my best endeavour is to be as sparing as I can. I shall be obliged to make a coat for the Emperor's arrival, and the one I made at Naples will serve to make me magnificent. I believe mournings will never be at an end; we shall now be obliged to mourn for the Duke of York, who, I hear, is certainly dead.

The Duke of York was, in fact, dead. His death had taken place at Monaco on 17 September, as the result of a chill caught at a dance. The papers published pathetic accounts of his death. He had written a letter to his brother, the King, expressing his unhappiness at their having parted on bad terms, which the King read with emotion.

William, however, was not concerned with the late Duke of York. His thoughts were occupied with his own affairs – with the weather, and the effect it had had on his own health:

We have had the most sudden change of weather that ever was, from being quite hot and being obliged to wear silk, it is grown all of a sudden as cold as ever I felt in the middle of winter. I have caught cold by not having any warm clothes with me. I went to bed last night not at all [well], but this morning I am much better; but I rather lay abed too long to have the pleasure of writing you a longer letter, as the post is just going, so I must conclude by assuring you how much I am your most affectionate son, KILDARE. Your dear picture is amazingly admired by everybody here, but they won't believe it is my Mother's.

Some time after the previous July, William had sent to his mother an account* of his first year's expenses. This document had evidently

* Not extant.

caused his parents surprise – and consternation; for we now find William, on his return to Florence, writing as follows:

Florence, October the 3rd, 1767. My dearest Mother, I received your letter of the 5th of September, which has caused a great uneasiness in my mind, in regard to the Duke not being content with my conduct in regard to money matters. I own at the time I drew I always thought that my money was going too fast, but at the same time you must consider I set out from England almost naked. I had but the coat upon my back and another. As for stockings, dress ruffles, etc., etc., I had none. When you come to look into those articles one must see that all that is necessary. As to servants and carriages, etc., I can assure you they are not more than necessary; you must consider one must have a carriage, coachmen and footman that knows the town. Carriages are very dear in Italy; so much so that when I go into small towns such as Lucca, etc., I never had a carriage. At Rome and Naples I believe I mentioned in a former letter that I lost playing at loo very near a hundred pounds.

In short, my dear Mother, there are so many necessary articles that a young man wants at setting out in the world.

I can assure you when I sent the account of the yearly expense, it hurt me very much; and since then I have been determined to be as careful as possible. And I promise you that I'll not dawdle it away, for I should look upon myself as very ungrateful if I did not do everything in my power to oblige and serve so good a Father as mine.

As to the voyage to Vienna, that came a little abruptly, as I had flattered myself with the thoughts of spending this winter in Italy. But, to be sure, the Duke's reasons are very good, and I shall take care during my whole stay there to make the army my chief study. What disturbs me is your mentioning the setting off immediately. I hope that my reasons will convince the Duke that it is not through neglect, or disobedience, that I do not set off immediately; but as I am to go Vienna, in my opinion it will be better to stay here till the Emperor comes. By that means I shall be presented to him here, and as he is very attentive to the English it'll be of more service to me at Vienna. Also, it'll be in my power to make acquaintance with some of his attendants, and with Mr. Rosenbergh's letters I make no doubt but I shall spend my time very well. The Emperor is expected in 3 weeks, so you see it delays my journey but a little while. During the time he goes to Rome, Naples, etc., etc., I shall go to Turin and follow him to Vienna, which will be about Christmas. Till then it'll hardly be possible to get to Vienna, as he travels with such a train. By which means, if the Duke is content, I sincerely wish this scheme may please the Duke, as I can assure you that I should be the most unhappy man living if I thought myself ever guilty of disobliging my father.

I must also let you into the secret that I have bought a coat, before I received yours, on purpose for his Imperial Majesty. I hope you are thoroughly convinced it is not any mark of disrespect that I am guilty of in not putting your orders into direct execution, as really them are my reasons ... P.S. I shall be in daily expectation for an answer to set my mind at rest and assure me I have not acted contrary to your will.

The enormous expenses that William had incurred clearly caused him great distress. But it is equally clear that they were unavoidable. First, there was the cost of travel itself: posting in Italy was very expensive. Then there was the retinue of attendants that a man of rank was obliged to employ – his running footmen, his valet, and other servants – William was careful in this respect, he employed one regular servant, 'and a footman which I take in the town' – there was the coach he had to keep in every large town; there were the clothes he must wear – the suits of silk and velvet and lace; the dinners he had to give in return for the hospitality he received; the expensive hotels he might have to stay in until he found furnished lodgings; the large tips that must be given to the servants whenever a visit was made either at a private house, or to a cardinal in Rome, or to a concert or a party – the greater the visitor's rank the more was expected from him; the betting and gambling that was the usual form of entertainment amongst the nobility, and which even William, despite all his efforts, had been unable entirely to avoid; the hairdresser – in Paris gentlemen's hair was dressed every day.

It seems, indeed, that William managed on less than some of his contemporaries. His friend, Lord Carlisle, wrote from Naples the following year (1768): 'These cursed feasts will ruin me in servants. I am forced to have seven here, and have another on the road. Though I hope soon to dismiss some of mine, yet the house cannot well be too large, as we shall not have less than thirteen or fourteen servants.' And Charles Fox while abroad gambled away a large part of his father's fortune. Gibbon, it may be remembered, drew £900 for a year in Switzerland and Italy.

It was exceedingly difficult for a young Englishman making the Grand Tour to live cheaply. Everything was against him. The inhabitants of Italy and France regarded him as legitimate prey. And it was understandable. For generations England had been the wealthiest country in Europe. Added to which young English travellers had squandered their riches in order to impress foreigners: they had been known to throw money from the windows for the fun of collecting a crowd! Early in the century Lady Mary Wortley Montagu had commented: 'I know how far people are imposed on that bear the name of English and heretics into the bargain; the folly of British boys, and stupidity and knavery of governors, have gained us the glorious title of Golden Asses all over Italy.' Is it any wonder that the English were considered so rich that they were made to pay double for everything in every country?

Florence, October the 10th, 1767. I hope you received my last letter of the 3rd instant, wherein I mention my reasons for not setting out directly. I hope they'll convince the Duke and you that it is not through neglect I do not obey your orders so punctually as I should have done. The Emperor is expected very soon; there are already some of his people arrived. I forgot to mention to you how well the sea bathing agreed with me. I also was at Lucca some time. I cannot say it is an agreeable town at all. There was a lady and her daughter there I visited; the former was the picture of Mrs. Letablere and the daughter very like Lady Cecilia.

We have charming weather, neither too hot nor cold. The Grand Duke is going to Leghorn for a day to see the Maltese galleys. I believe I shall take a trip over there too, as I am told they are very well worth seeing, and then I shall see them to great advantage as they are to go through all their manoeuvres for the Duke. It would be a pity to miss so good an occasion ... The post goes out at a very inconvenient hour, and my dancing master is waiting, so I must beg of you to present my love to the Duke ... etc. Your vases are not yet finished; I hope they'll please you.

Florence, Saturday, October 17th, 1767. Since my last of the 10th instant, is arrived the account of the Queen of Naples having the smallpox, which puts a stop to the Emperor's coming here till spring; for which reason I set off for Turin on Wednesday, where I shall make a longer stay than I should have done otherwise. If you should have any other schemes in your head about my proceeding, I should be much obliged to you to let me know them. I own I am very sorry to leave Italy so soon, especially without seeing Genoa, Milan and Venice; but it is to be hoped I shall see them next year, at least your letter seems to flatter my hopes. Your vases will not be finished till December; they are to be sent to Leghorn as soon as they are finished, and sent the first opportunity that offers to Dublin. I flatter myself they'll please you.

Pray, tell the Duke that I have no letter of credit upon Vienna. Also

> if he could procure me a letter for Lord Stormont; as I know all the Ambassadors and Ministers like that the people should bring them letters of recommendation, especially when you are not acquainted with them.

David Murray, 7th Viscount Stormont, who succeeded his uncle as 2nd Earl of Mansfield in 1793, was Ambassador at Vienna from 1763 to 1772. Before this he had been Envoy to Warsaw; later he became Ambassador at Paris.

> Our weather has been very indifferent lately; a great deal of rain, which will make our roads through Lombardy very indifferent. Charles Fox goes with me as far as Turin in his way to Montauban to meet Lord and Lady Holland ... Direct to me chez Mess. Torras, Banquiers, at Turin.

Lord and Lady Holland were on the point of leaving England for Paris *en route* for Nice, where they were to spend the winter on account of Lord Holland's asthma.

And now William was about to leave the home of his ancestors. Soon the streets and squares of Florence would be only a memory. The swift-flowing Arno, the Ponte Vecchio, the Piazza della Signoria, the churches and the palazzi, the narrow streets that had felt the tread of Savanarola's sandals and Machiavelli's sinewy slippers, Ghiberti's golden doors and the cold marble of the duomo, Verrocchio's Dolphin Boy flitting across the dim courtyard of the Palazzo Vecchio, the still cypresses standing in the sharp sunlight of the Boboli gardens, the gently falling water of the fountains, the brilliant flowers heaped in every alleyway, the sliced melon sold in the streets, the Raphaels and the Titians, Brunelleschi's exquisite Pazzi Chapel, the ancient Tower of the Gherardini – all these and more William would see for the last time.

There was no longer any reason for William to remain in Florence. The Queen of Naples had smallpox; the Emperor had postponed his visit. Presently came the news that the Queen of Naples had died. The Court went into mourning.

Once more William stepped into the carriage with his cousin, Charles Fox. It was a little over a year since the two had set out together from Paris on the road to Lyons. Now, accompanied as always by Mr Bolle, they turned their horses towards the steep climb over the Apennines, in the direction of Bologna. Driving between the conical hills, the scattered white houses of the nobility, the golden vines, the groves of olive and cypress – hurrying along the road past low carts drawn by white Virgilian oxen – they no doubt interrupted their animated conversation to turn and look down at the red tiled roofs of the city; the red tiled dome – outlined in white marble – of the duomo; the Campanile; the many towers; the river caught in the October sun. And when they reached the post house at the summit, with nothing in sight but the grand slopes of the Etruscan Apennines, the air chill, and perhaps a veil of mist suspended in the valley below, it must have been with some feelings of regret that the two young men turned their backs on the graceful land of Tuscany and started their descent into Emilia.

— 6 —

TURIN – NICE – TURIN

William reached Turin in four days. This was quite good going. But it must be remembered that Italian postillions drove very fast, trotting up hills, galloping on the level. Neither was Charles Fox given to dawdling; and we may be sure that he and William gave their postillion every encouragement to cover the ground as quickly as possible.

Ringed by the Alps, the Piedmontese capital had only recently been raised, stone upon stone, to form one of the loveliest of European cities. 'Its beauties,' writes Mr Jasper More, 'are contemporary with our own city of London, and its culture is of the same quality as that brought back by Charles II from his French exile. Turin, in fact, is the creation of an emancipated prince, inspired by the glories of Louis XIV and Versailles, the Italian counterpart of Darmstadt or Dresden; and in contrast to the mass of artistic inspiration which through the centuries has flowed from Italy to France, it may be considered the principal gift of the French artistic inspiration to Italy.'*

Eighteenth-century opinions of the city differed. Some travellers thought the place dull; others admired the regular network of broad straight boulevards, flanked by arcades and planted with pleasant avenues of trees, and the arcaded squares with their elegant palaces. William was immediately impressed with the town and leaves us in no doubt as to his preference for the later styles of architecture over the medieval.

William's first letter from Turin is sealed with a black seal, in mourning for the Queen of Naples.

> Turin, the 27th of October, 1767. My dearest Mother, According to my Father's desire, I set out for Turin the day after the news came of the Queen of Naples's death, seeing there no hopes of the Emperor coming to Florence. I arrived here after a journey of 4 days through a fine country, though I cannot say a very beautiful, as it is such a dead

---

* *The Land of Italy* (Batsford) p. 87.

flat from Bologna to within a few posts of this. Charles Fox came with me. He is going to Montauban to meet Lord and Lady Holland. I own I am very much grieved at leaving Italy without seeing Genoa, Venice, Milan, etc., etc. Also, I left Florence very unwillingly, as I spent my time very well, having a great many acquaintances and talking the beautiful Tuscan language, which, to be sure, is the most beautiful of all languages. The people that have been here do not give me a good account of this place, but I do not believe them; and I make no doubt but I shall amuse myself very well for the short time I stay here. I have not yet been presented at Court, as our Chargé d'Affaires is not well; but if he does not recover soon, I shall find some other means of being presented. I dread the journey to Vienna, as it is in a very bad season; and I shall find it a very *triste* Court. I expected to have passed the winter at the Academy here, which would have been a very [great] economy and, by what I hear, not disagreeable; and the masters are very good; and then to have seen the rest of Italy in spring and to have spent the summer at Vienna. I spoke to Count Rosanberg, who promised to send me a letter the day before I left Florence, but the melancholy news of the Queen's death arrived that day [and] he was obliged to be at Court. She died the day she was to have been married by proxy. I, by way of being an economist, made up my coat, which I have packed up carefully, as it will be a good coat for when the mourning is out at Vienna, as they dress very richly there. We have a great loss in not having Mr Pitt here or some other minister, as a minister generally adds a great deal to society; and it is always a place where one may go when one has nothing else to do.

George Pitt had been appointed Envoy to Turin in 1761. He arrived here in March 1762; he left on leave two years later, and did not return, although his appointment continued until 1768. He was later created Baron Rivers. His wife, Penelope, was a famous beauty, celebrated in Walpole's poem on *The Beauties*. Nevertheless, Walpole declared William's mother, who was her contemporary, to be even more beautiful.

As for the beauties of this place I can [not] give you any account of [them] as I have not yet seen them. The town is much the handsomest I have seen in Italy, as the houses are regularly built and the streets are wide; it is but a small town. I forgot to mention this is the 2nd or 3rd time Charles Fox has been here for to meet Lord Carlisle, who, I believe, has no thoughts of coming this way, though he is to have his green ribbon here. But that is not yet come.

Frederick Howard, 5th Earl of Carlisle, was nineteen years old. He was made Knight of the Thistle on 23 December, 1767, being invested at Turin by the King of Sardinia on 27 February the following year.

On their return from making the Grand Tour Carlisle and Charles Fox were considered to be the two best-dressed men in London society. Carlisle later filled various important posts, including that of Lord Lieutenant of Ireland. He was closely related to Byron, whose guardian he became.

> Travelling in this part of Italy is monstrous dear. I believe to make up for my travelling expenses (that causes me more uneasiness than one can imagine) you must marry me to Miss FitzGerald as soon as I return; so I beg you'll make Cecilia and Emily pay their court to her whenever they see her. I like the description that Cecilia sent me very well, and I think there is no time to lose, as I hear they want to marry Master King to her directly, and it would be a thousand pities that poor William should lose so good a match. (I am in earnest) ...
>
> ... Charles Fox, I believe, begs to be remembered to the Duke and you, but I dare not disturb him as he is writing to his *Cicisbea* at Florence.
>
> Since I wrote this I have just received a letter from Lady Cecilia of the 25th of September. Pray, my love to Mrs Lyons, and tell her to keep her hand in in the caudle way against the Marchioness lies in.(*sic*)

Caroline FitzGerald, it will be recalled, was heiress to a fortune worth more than £6,000 a year. William's rival for her hand was her cousin, the thirteen-year-old Robert King. William seems to have been very optimistic that the 'courting' of the young lady by his aunt and his sister would be successful. His thoughts were indeed travelling a long way ahead; Mrs Lyons was a midwife, and William, Marquess of Kildare, was looking forward to the time when there would be a Marchioness in the family needing the attention and the good warm gruel of a Mrs Lyons.

Meanwhile in faraway Dublin an event had taken place which was to enable William to take his first step in the political life of the city: the Recorder, James Grattan, had died. He had been Member of Parliament for the City of Dublin, and his death caused a by-election. William was chosen as a candidate, and was opposed by John La Touche, the Dublin banker.

4th November, 1767. My dearest Mother, I received your obliging letter of the 29th of September, wherin you mention the citizens of Dublin having done us the honour of desiring me to represent them in Parliament. I am of your opinion that it is much better staying abroad and finishing my travels at once now they are begun, than to take them at twice. I could wish to finish my tour of Italy before I went to Germany. I shall find Vienna in a very *triste* situation, as there is another of the Archduchesses that has got the smallpox.

Turin seems to be an agreeable place enough, but unless a person stays some time the people do not care to make acquaintance with you. I have been presented at Court, and was yesterday out a hunting with the King and royal family. We had a very good chase of a stag; it is amazing to see the King, who is sixty-seven years old, ride like a young man of 20. He is a very good-natured old man and talks to everybody.

The King was Charles Emmanuel III, King of Sardinia and head of the house of Savoy. This man, a good soldier and keen sportsman, was ancestor of the family which eventually came to reign over a united Italy. Descending in an unbroken male line from Humbert the White-Handed, they very early added to their original territory of the Count of Savoy, by acquiring part of Piedmont, including Turin. When in the sixteenth century the reigning Duke made Turin his capital city, the family interests became identified more with those of Italy than of France. During the first third of the eighteenth century Victor Amadeus II, one of the House of Savoy's greatest dukes and father of Charles Emmanuel III, rescued his country from internal strife and foreign invasion, making it for the first time a compact self-contained state. He was also successful in acquiring Sardinia with its royal title. Although the Dukes of Savoy were now known under the title of Kings of Sardinia, they continued to reside at Turin, which remained their capital. Much later, through the Risorgimento, they were to become Kings of Italy. But to return to Charles Emmanuel III: he had succeeded his father Victor Amadeus II, who abdicated, in 1730 – and he lived on until 1773.

My letters that I brought here have been very useful to me; but I brought a letter for one of the most agreeable ladies here, who is since dead; which is a great loss, as she had a great deal of *conversazione* for strangers. I could spend my winter very agreeably here. The most disagreeable thing is they have a language here which is neither Italian or French, but between both. The weather begins to be very cold. Especially the mornings and evenings.

Charles Fox left this Saturday. He must have had fine cold weather

77

crossing the Alps, as the snow begins to fall upon the mountains. It'll be very bad passing in a month hence.

I am very happy at your getting Charles a tutor, but I hope he continues mending.

William's last sentence refers to his brother, Lord Charles FitzGerald's, new tutor, Mr William Ogilvie; the very same Mr William Ogilvie, who, after the death of the Duke of Leinster, became, in 1774, Emily Duchess of Leinster's second husband. Ogilvie was now 27 years old.

11th of November, 1767. We had great change of weather since my last of the 4th of this month, as it is grown amazingly cold. I do not know but it appears to me to be as cold as ever I felt it in England; that may be owing to my having been this year past in so warm a climate. To be sure, last winter was hardly to be called a winter.

I have been out a hunting with the King, and the Duke of Savoy and his brother. I was told it was a proper compliment to ask leave to wear the hunting uniform, as the King is very fond that the English should hunt with him. By wearing the uniform you breakfast with the King and the royal family; it is quite a hunting breakfast, as he and the rest of the people eat standing with a plate and napkin in one hand and help oneself to whatever one likes. The king is a very civil good sort of an old gentleman, loves the English and hates the French, which I have not the worse opinion of him for so doing. The Duke of Savoy is a most amiable Prince, very civil and easy with everybody; he is adored here. The Duke of Chablais, his brother, who is reckoned proud here, I like him very much as, in my opinion, he is far from proud, as he speaks with everybody and has been remarkably civil to me. I follow him generally a hunting.

The Duke of Savoy was the eldest and only surviving son of the King by his second wife. The Duke was now 42 years old. His wife was daughter of Philip V of Spain. In 1773, on his father's death, he succeeded to the throne of Sardinia as Victor Amadeus III. The Duke of Chablais was the King's son by his third wife. Aged 26, he was a great favourite with his father. A few years later he married his niece, Maria Anna, who was daughter of his half-brother, the Duke of Savoy.

By what I hear there are excellent masters here for all sorts; it is a very good place for an Englishman to learn fortification, as the English only are permitted to see their works, this town being vastly well fortified.

I hear Lord Holland is determined to spend the winter at Nice. By what I hear it is quite an English town, as there are quantities there for their health. By all accounts, it is a most charming climate.

Nice was already becoming known to English people for its climate. Early in the century Dr Thomas Linolett had discovered its attractions; and from 1763 to 1765 Tobias Smollett, suffering from consumption, had spent about eighteen months there. Nice and the surrounding district had since its earliest times suffered successive invasions, and had several times changed hands. During the fifteenth and sixteenth centuries it belonged to Savoy, and again during the greater part of the eighteenth century. It had early connections with the House of Savoy, for Humbert the White-Handed was a descendant of Boson of Provence. The town and county of Nice at present (1767) formed part of the King of Sardinia's territories.

Encouraged by the anglophile King and his ministers, William's army studies were now in full swing:

November the 17th, 1767. My dearest Mother, I beg you'll make my excuse to Emily, as I owe her a letter which was to have been answered last post; but I was all morning at the Citadel seeing the fortifications, and the evening I was obliged to go and make a visit to return the Secretary of War thanks. I hope the Duke was not displeased at my having the King's hunting uniform, as I was informed before that he and the Duke of Savoy like to see the English. Not only that, but it makes you in a manner acquainted with all the first people here, as it is not every Piedmontese that has leave to wear it. At the same time it gives one an opportunity of seeing a great deal of the Duke of Savoy and his brother, who are two most amiable Princes; they are very obliging, free and easy. I have a good number of acquaintances here, and but two English, which is not disagreeable, as the hours that one does not go into company, there is no English to come and disturb one in one's studies. I am grown much fonder of reading than I used to be, which is a great happiness; not only useful, but it has almost broke me of that bad trick I had of dawdling away my time. I now often repent I did not apply myself more to lecture in my younger days. One comfort, it'll make me enjoy our winter evenings at Carton with more pleasure than I did formerly.

I hope you, or one of your young secretaries, will give me some account of the election. Pray, is it true that the city have presented me with the freedom of the city in a gold box, as the English paper mentions?

Our weather is cold and damp at present. The mountains are almost covered with snow, a good pleasant sight when I think of the journey that I am to make; I could wish it was delayed till spring, for Turin is a very agreeable town, and I could perfect myself a little more in fortification, etc.; for at Vienna they are very strict about letting people see into their military affairs.

'Turin is a very agreeable town.' We only need to consider the period at which the city was built, and the architects employed in the building, to appreciate the truth of William's remark. Most of the important buildings were completed during the 170 years following upon Turin becoming the ducal capital in 1563. Towards the end of the seventeenth century Guarini working here; it was he designed the Carignano royal palace, built of red brick in the Piedmontese baroque style. Amongst his many other buildings is the chapel of the Santa Sindone wedged on a high platform between the cathedral and the royal palace. Guarini's successor, Juvara, was employed in Turin during the early years of the eighteenth century. He too worked in the Piedmontese baroque style, and his baroque and rococo is always light and pleasing. He did a great deal of his finest work outside the city. Most splendid of all his achievements is the Superga, a domed basilica of white stone standing in the Turinese Hills overlooking Turin and the surrounding plain. The Superga (1731) was built for Victor Amadeus II in expiation of a vow made during the siege of the city by the French in 1706. The vault beneath the church contains the tombs of members of the royal family. Royal residences dot the countryside. One of these is Stupinigi, also by Juvara., a hunting lodge built in the rococo style. This may have been the lodge from which William hunted with the King and his family.

William was now making his plans for the immediate future. Clearly his own wish was to remain on in Turin for the winter; he had, indeed, said so. But, as obliging a son as ever, he prepared to fall in with his father's desire that he should continue his journey to Vienna without delay. It is very probable that, in faraway Ireland, the Duke of Leinster, in spite of having made the Grand Tour himself in his youth, had no true conception of travelling conditions in central Europe at this time of year. The Austrian roads were bad; in winter many were impassable. And so, with the thoughts of a terrible journey before him, William sat down and wrote to his mother:

November 25th, 1767. I was much pleased with your obliging letter of the 23rd October, which made me, as you may imagine, very happy finding that I had not disobliged the Duke by staying at Florence in expectation of the Emperor. But, finding that the journey was delayed, I set off for Turin, as the Duke seemed desirous of my seeing it before I left Italy. I find by your letter that he seems determined that I should spend the remaining part of the winter at Vienna, for which reason I propose leaving this in about ten days, by which means I shall be there by January or the latter end of next month, as I shall stop but two days at Milan and one at Verona. I shall then proceed over the Alps, which are as whiteheaded as General Sandford, a good comfortable prospect for a traveller.

I read your letter to Bolle. We are determined to be as saving as we can, I can assure you. As for servants, I have had but the one I took with me, and a footman which I take in the town, as it is very necessary. I shall now be obliged to take a man who can talk German, as neither I, Bolle or my own footman can talk it; he is a Vienna man, for which reasons he serves me for a *lacque de louage* at Vienna. I can assure my dear Mother I should look upon myself as very ungrateful if I did not do everything that lies in my power to oblige so obliging a Father and Mother. I can assure you that it shall be my best endeavours to be as saving as it is possible. But tell the honest truth, which is that the Italians have such notions of every Englishman being a *Lord Clive*, and think it is impossible for an Englishman to pay enough; for, to be sure, the follies that the English are guilty of in regard to money are enough to turn the heads of anybody that has to do with them. I must also mention one thing in regard to eating, which is the English at Florence and Rome, though living in the same house, was always for giving dinners; so a course one was obliged to return. At Florence I was very sparing, seeing into the follies of it; at Rome I must own that I kept a very good table, but I have been determined not to keep table any more while I am abroad.

William's reference to Robert Clive, the famous general, who had amassed a vast fortune in India, and his other remarks in the foregoing letter, provide further evidence for the difficulties experienced by the English tourist who tried to travel economically.

I yesterday received an account of your carnation roots being sent to Leghorn, and to be embarked for Dublin the 1st opportunity that offers; I am told that they are of the best sort. Great cautions are to be given to the Captain, so I am in hopes you'll receive them safe. I have writ to Leghorn that as soon as ever they are put on board, that the bill of lading should be sent to Mr Bere.* Pray, my love to the Duke, and the rest of the family, not forgetting the young ladies, to whom I sent the Pope's blessing for writing so often. How does the election go on? ... P.S. I do not mean by keeping a good table that I kept open house.

The beginning of December arrived. William was still worrying about his projected journey to Vienna over the snow-covered roads. Indeed, his dread mounted almost to panic:

December 2nd, 1767. Our last post having missed, I have not had any account of my election. I should be very happy to hear of its being over ... I do not know what sort of weather you have, but ours is charming and frosty, as it freezes very hard every night, and the mountains covered with snow. Pleasant prospect for a traveller! People here reckoned me mad when I mentioned my journey to Vienna. I own I dread it, as [it is] a fortnight's journey. I shall not stop anywhere till I get there, as the Duke seems so desirous that I should spend my winter there. As to the sea bathing, I must give up the thoughts of that for some time. I hope you'll remember that I have not seen Venice, Bologna, Milan and Genoa, and that I have been but a little while here. Lord Stormont has left Vienna, which is a loss, as all places are worse when there is no minister or ambassador, especially at Vienna where there is so much etiquette.

As William's pen raced over the paper, he clutched wildly at any straw that would save him from the dreaded journey; and jotted down every possible reason he could think of for not proceeding. His thoughts turned longingly to the pleasant climate of Nice; and he envied the Hollands who had already arrived there for the winter. The Hollands, who had spent the summer in England, had set out towards the end of October, taking Harry with them, who on and off had been ill at Eton. In Paris they met Charles, who had come from Italy to meet them. On their arrival at Nice, the Hollands found the town, as they had expected – and indeed as they had hoped – quiet.

Lord Holland, I believe, is arrived at Nice, as I saw a gentleman that came from thence the other day, told me he was expected every day. I own I felt sorry at the thoughts of leaving Turin, as I have made a great many acquaintances, and there being so few English and the thoughts of a journey over mountains covered with snow, the bad inns, etc., make me wish it over. I do not know how you are to direct to me at

* Under-agent to the Duke of Leinster.

Vienna, as I have not yet got my letter of credit for Vienna.

All this uncomfortable travelling was getting William down. He let out a last despairing cry:

> I hope you'll make the young ladies be civil to Miss FitzGerald upon all occasions, as I wish I was married to her and settled.

Condemned as he believed himself to be to a most terrible journey, William made one more effort to free himself. An idea struck him; it was a ray of hope. Was it his own ideas, or did the good Mr Bolle suggest it? We shall never know. In any case, two days after his last letter home, he sat down and wrote to his aunt, Lady Holland, at Nice. He did not ask her anything. He simply stated facts. And he left it to her, an experienced traveller who knew the conditions of continental roads well enough to imagine his plight. He might stir her pity. The following is what he wrote to his aunt:

> Friday the 4th [December], 1767. My dear Lady, I was informed by a gentleman who came from Nice that you and Lord Holland were expected every day, so I presume you are there by this time; so I take this 1st opportunity of writing to enquire after yours and Lord Holland's health and how he has borne his journey. I am in great hopes this winter at Nice will entirely establish him. I hope your weather is not so cold as ours, as it is dreadfully cold here; we have had snow and frost for some time, pleasant weather for to set out for Vienna. I own I set out much against my will, not only to leave Turin and Italy, but I dread a fortnight's journey, as I have not time to stop anywhere till I get to Vienna. I was in hopes to have made you a visit, but I am afraid I must give up all thoughts of it. I hope you'll be so kind as to let me know how Lord Holland does, directing me a line to Mess. Torras á Turin. My love to my Lord, Charles and Harry. I am, my dearest Aunt, your most affectionate nephew, KILDARE.

While awaiting his aunt's reply, William caught a cold, which turned to influenza. The days crept by. His thoughts were very much centred upon the Dublin election, which had taken place on 28 November. But posts were slow in coming, and he still had not heard the result.

> December the 9th, 1767. My dearest Mother, I have this very day been

favoured with your obliging [letter] of the 8th of November, and am also much obliged to Mr Ward for his note, where he seems to think there is no doubt of his success. I must own I have set my heart upon it too much, knowing Mr Latouche's interest and having received a letter from a friend of his, who mentioned his being determined to stand at the election. He has one great advantage, which is that of his being rich. I own that I should be very happy if I succeed. I knew of Mr Connolly being engaged, but Mr Andrews was not. It is very kind of him to remember me, as we lived a great deal together at Naples, and Rome, especially at Rome, as we lived over against one another. For the time I was confined with my breaking out, and that I did [not] go into company, he used to come or I went to him ...

The 'Mr Andrews' mentioned was Francis Andrews, Provost of Trinity College, Dublin.

I should have been on my road now had not I been detained by a small cold and cough, but I shall set out in a few days. I shall be obliged to draw for some money to bear my expenses there, and I am in hopes you'll find that I have been very moderate since I have been here. You may depend upon my being as moderate as it is possible. I name this place as one when I return into Italy, but there is time enough to think of that, but I have a very good route in my head ... I must now beg leave to mention one thing in regard to expense. I have met with a gentleman lately who is come here from Vienna, [who] says it is one of the most expensive places abroad. You have been misinformed about the gambling here, as it is forbid here as well as in most other courts in Italy.

Five days later William was in high spirits. His hopes had been fulfilled – the journey to Vienna was off! Lady Holland's reply to him has not come down to us. But it is quite clear that in her letter she invited him to stay with her at Nice instead of proceeding to Vienna. It is equally clear that she took the whole responsibility of this change of plan upon herself. It must have been with a feeling of relief that William wrote the following letter to his mother:

December 14th, 1767. I have just time to write a few lines to let you know that I am very well, and have got the better of my *grippe*, which is the new fashioned cold here; there are about 12,000 people ill of it; nobody dies, so you may not be uneasy about me. Bolle is quite well again. We set out for Nice tomorrow. It is two days and a half journey. I shall be able, I hope, to send you a good account of Lord and Lady Holland. It is by her desire that I go, or else tomorrow was the day fixed for Germany; but Lady Holland promises to bear the blame, so that I hope you will not think it my negligence. I long to hear how the election finishes, though I have not set my heart upon it, as Mr Latouche's being so rich, and having applied before. I hope my dearest Mother will excuse of the shortness of this letter and accept it from her most affectionate son, KILDARE. My love to the Duke, etc., etc., etc. I wish you all a Merry Xmas.

Turin to Nice was a distance of about 30 leagues (90 miles) over the mountains; the only method of making the precipitous journey was by mule, or by chair.

William arrived safely at Nice, and was soon happily installed there with his uncle and aunt. His first letter from there was written two days before Christmas:

NICE, the 23rd of December, 1767. My dearest Mother, I arrived here last week and was much pleased in finding Lord and Lady Holland so well. Lord Holland is better than [when] he left Naples. To be sure, this is a charming climate. They tell me I have seen the worst of it, as the 2 or 3 days past have been but indifferent. Mr William Clements is here also; he says he finds himself better, but, poor man, he can't walk without the help of a man; he looks very well in the face. Lord Farnham is here also, for his health; he seems to think that the air has done him good, I should have bathed in the sea, but they say the weather was too cold to begin, and as I have not quite got rid of my *grippe* or cold.

I was made very happy by receiving an account of my being chosen member for the city of Dublin. By all accounts it must have cost a great deal of money, which I think is the worst part of it, as at present money will be still scarcer than it was, so I am determined to be a great economist.

At last William had heard the good news of his having been elected Member of Parliament for the City of Dublin. In spite of all his riches, the banker La Touche had been defeated. The polling had lasted eighteen days, and the contest had been severe – William's majority being only 137. His election was no doubt largely a tribute to the popularity of his patriot father, the Duke. William, however, could not take his seat as he was not yet of age. So he did not interrupt his travels.

William confided to the Hollands his hopes of marrying Miss FitzGerald. They listened, and – approved. 'Pray,' William begged his mother, 'desire them [his aunt Cecilia and sister Emily] to be civil to Miss FitzGerald, as I think seriously about her, and Lord and Lady Holland think it right.' Indeed, Lady Holland wrote to her sister the Duchess, saying she hoped, if it proved necessary for William to return to Ireland on account of his election that 'I shall soon hear he is to marry Miss FitzGerald. Lord Holland is quite eager about it; so am I, because William is; and that I think, as far as those worldly considerations, very desirous.' 'Lord Holland is wild about the FitzGerald match'; she added a little later, 'you know how eager and impatient he is to bring about anything he thinks desirable; he wants you to send for him immediately. I am most exceedingly for the match because William himself is; but I think the Duke of Leinster and you upon the spot must know how far it may be necessary to hasten it immediately.' In his eagerness for the match, Lord Holland was running true to form. He had been desperately anxious when his sister-in-law, Lady Sarah Lennox, was a young girl, that she should marry the 22-year-old George III, his ambitions had only been thwarted by the determination of the Dowager Princess of Wales and the Earl of Bute. Although in the case of Miss FitzGerald a royal mother and a statesman-tutor were not the adversaries, adversaries there certainly were. As has already been said, Caroline FitzGerald's cousin, thirteen-year-old Master King, was in the running for her hand; and his relations were doing all they could to organise the match. 'There was,' continued Lady Holland, 'a Colonel Holmes here, a friend of the Marquess, who informed him how likely it was she might already be engaged to the Kings, who would take certain measures to secure her in their family. The Marquess is so meek and so obliging a temper, he will make almost any woman happy, and not easily let her disturb him. I really wish it of all things.'

William's thoughts were much occupied with Miss FitzGerald. He turned the subject over and over in his mind. The more he thought of it, the more suitable he thought the marriage would be. Miss FitzGerald was very rich indeed. From all accounts she seemed to be a most agreeable girl. He was sure he could make her happy. And as for her money – he could turn that to very good account, for he had a great many brothers and sisters, and one day he would have to provide for them all. It would be no use marrying a penniless girl, however attractive. No, Miss FitzGerald was too good an opportunity to miss. But his family seemed to be dilly-dallying over the affair, and urging him to stay abroad, when he should be getting back to make his formal offer to the girl. Would they never take him seriously? His aunt, Lady Holland, in whom he confided, understood his feelings perfectly. The marriage would, she had assured him, make him 'the greatest subject almost in Europe'. As Lady Holland walked round the ramparts that over-looked the district surrounding Nice, discussing the matter with her husband, she became more and more convinced of the desirability of the match. It was not that William, she argued, would ever do any-thing scrubby or shabby, but he had a proper regard for money, and seemed to have no extravagant turn at all. He was not in the slightest degree childish, his character was formed, and he seemed to know his own mind very well. She thought it very lucky that he was so eager about it. But she realised he was very much afraid of Master King, in spite of his being so young; for he knew that Colonel Holmes' authority was very good. Poor William! He felt so helpless at such a distance. At last his aunt agreed to write to his mother the Duchess and inform her of William's seriousness in the matter. The Duchess' reply revealed her reason for not being keen on the marriage. Miss FitzGerald, she said, was *too young* to marry. When Lady Holland read this out to her husband, he became very agitated. He pressed his wife to write back to the Duchess to remind her that their mother, Sarah, 2nd Duchess of Richmond, was married at thirteen, and that their father travelled afterwards. 'What, then,' asked Lord Holland, 'becomes of the Duchess's expression, *la chose qui n'est pas possible?*' As for William's rival, Master King, Harry Fox gives a picture of him a little later when they were both at Eton: he never saw, he said, an ugli-er little monkey in his life; and that he acted quite like a child. But for all that, warned Lady Holland, unless the Duke of Leinster out-bids him, she feared he would get Miss FitzGerald from the Marquess.

William spent Christmas at Nice. He was thoroughly enjoying his visit to his uncle and aunt, both of whom were well and in good spirits. They had some bad weather; but on the whole the climate was charming. William infinitely preferred it to that of Naples, which was subject to sudden change. Here at Nice, on the last day of December, the oranges were still upon the trees, the roses and jessamin were still in bloom. Besides the Hollands and William, the party consisted of the two Fox boys, Charles and Harry, and Lord Carlisle. So at last Lord Carlisle had arrived! At last he had torn himself away from the lovely Lady Sarah Bunbury, upon whom he had been dancing atten-dance for some time. How often had Charles Fox been to Turin to meet him in vain? Now Lord Carlisle had reached Nice – accompanied, from Paris, by Charles Fox – and soon he would proceed to Turin to receive his Order of the Thistle at the hands of the King of Sardinia. Charles must have been very happy to have Carlisle at last, for they were great friends, and almost the same age, Lord Carlisle being but one year older than Charles. In her letters Lady Holland confided to her sister her thoughts about Charles. He was, she declared, an amiable boy. Her only fear for him was that his indolence would get the better of his superior genius. She would not be content with his being only an amiable, sensible, agreeable man; she was glad that Charles could not indulge in gaming since that form of amusement was strictly forbidden in Nice. Lord Carlisle was a good sort of young man, much improved, and said he had quite left off gaming. He would, perhaps, be a good influence upon Charles.

William now heard that his mother wished him to stay some time longer at Turin when he returned there from Nice. He was glad of this, and assured her that he would make good use of the time spent there. By staying at Turin some time he would be better prepared for Vienna; and it would also be saving, as Turin was the cheapest place in Italy. He was very anxious to see both Milan and Genoa; and he wanted to be in Venice for the Ascension in May – Ascension time was the winding up of the Italian season of amusements for foreigners. The great fair in the Piazza of St Mark began with the Feast of the Ascension, and on Ascension Day the Doge wedded the Adriatic with his ring. Besides the out-of-door spectacles there were eight or nine theatres, including opera houses – after sea bathing at Venice, William intended to go on to Vienna. In this way he would have completed his tour of Italy, and it would not be necessary for him to return.

The new year came. The middle of January found William still at Nice. The weather had improved:

NICE, the 13th of January, 1768 ... This day is absolutely summer. I wish I could transport it to you. What fine weather we have had here; it is far superior to Naples. Altogether I prefer this climate to that of Naples. I flatter myself that towards next winter you'll think of me a little, as I can assure you my absence from you appears very long; though I can assure you that next to being with you being abroad is the most agreeable. Yet I own I begin to long to see you. I can assure you nobody is happier than I am abroad, and I have nothing to complain of ... Lord Carlisle and I propose setting off this day sennight for Turin. He goes to receive his green ribbon. I propose studying hard at Turin. The sea bathing and drinking has done me good, I believe it'll be necessary to get some more this year ... Lord Holland, thank God, continues well and in very good spirits, (he begs me to tell you that he thinks me much handsomer than ever you was, and his saying it makes Lady Holland peevish, as he says.) But he has been in violent spirits this week past.

A few days later William said goodbye to the Hollands, and, together with Lord Carlisle and Mr Bolle, set out along the mountain road back to Turin. 'I am to be carried,' wrote Lord Carlisle, 'two days' journey in a d----ed chair. The Marquis is too heavy; he therefore rides a mule.' On Wednesday 20 January they set off at 6 o'clock in the morning. They were soon in the Alps, travelling over rocks, and along frightening precipices. When darkness came their path was lit by torchlight. The first night they did not stop until ten o'clock. The following day William's muleteers and Carlisle's chairmen refused to pass the Col di Tenda, as the wind was too high and the snow was falling too thick. Luckily they had a recommendation to someone who lived nearby, with whom they stayed the night. The following day they reached the summit of the Col di Tenda. Descending in sledges they arrived that night by twelve o'clock at Coni, a fortified town in Piedmont 35 miles south of Turin. The next morning, by very good roads, which were well supplied with horses, they reached Turin itself. From Turin William wrote describing his journey:

> TURIN, 27th of January, 1768. I take this first opportunity of acquainting you of our safe arrival at Turin, after a journey of four days through valleys, over mountains covered with snow, etc. Though wrapped up in fur, it was cold. We came down the mountain upon *traineaus*; the snow was not frozen enough to go as quick as one generally does. Lord Carlisle came with me. He proposes staying a month or six weeks, as he is to receive his green ribbon here. He is an amiable young man. Don't be uneasy about his gaming, as I believe he means to drop that bad custom. He has never once proposed play to me, and you may be assured I shall never propose to him. I have been his introducer everywhere, as we have neither minister or *chargé d'affaires*. There being no Englishman here who has the King's entrée but me, I presented him at Court. (We were graciously received) ... I hope you'll excuse the shortness of this letter, as I have not yet made all my visits, and in the morning I was at Court.

Life for William at Turin continued very pleasantly. He and Lord
Carlisle were learning to dance cotillons. The carnival was in full
swing, with its dancing and feasting.

February 3rd, 1768 ... Upon my return to Turin and have taken up my
masters, I mean to apply myself very hard. At present the carnival has
caused some little irregularity, as there is balls or suppers almost every
night, which keeps one up. But as there is but a few days more, I shall
then return to my regular way of living, which is a very good article in
regard to one's health, as well as to its being agreeable. Tonight I am to
go to a *soupée dansant* at the French Ambassador's; he has already given
one which was very agreeable and pretty, as there was no crowd, and
none but dancers asked. We begin dancing as soon as the opera is over,
which is between ten and eleven o'clock and then we sup at one, then
dance after supper. At the last there were sixteen ladies, twelve of which
were Piedmontese, and I am sure ten of them might be reckoned pretty. I had the misfortune of treading on a lady's toe, which has caused
the talk of the town, though it is kept a secret from me, as the lady
knows I did not do it on purpose, and she desires that I should make
no apologies for it ...

    I do not ride at the King's riding house, as one must be of the acad-
emy; and when I first came I did not enter, as one is obliged to enter
for six months. You then intended my spending the winter in Vienna.
To be sure if one stays six months it is well worth one's while, especially as it is as cheap a way of living as any. At present we must be econo-
mists on account of the election and increase of the family. Pray, what
are the Duke's intentions whether I go to Germany or no? You know I
am willing to do just as he pleases, but by all accounts Vienna is a very
expensive place. I have some thoughts of Geneva or Lausanne, as I hear
they are both very agreeable. But the great fault is I doubt there be too
many English. But I shall just be guided as you and the Duke think
proper, as I am sure you are the best judges; and I only mention some
of them places as not quite so expensive as Germany, or else I should
not dislike taking the German journey next summer.

The weather was bitterly cold. The streets covered with ice, the houses with snow. The coming of the opera was enough 'to kill a
Laplander'.

Ash Wednesday, 1768. I can with pleasure assure you of my being perfectly recovered of my late indisposition, but still continue the flannel
waistcoat; that, I am afraid, I must continue the whole winter, which is

not at an end. Our carnival ended this morning at 7 o'clock. I regret the opera being finished, as it was an excellent place for seeing all the world.

The opera was magnificent. But, as at Naples, the people went to the opera mainly to visit their friends in their boxes. During the singing they made a great noise. It was only while the dancing was going on that they paid attention. The end of the Carnival brought tears to the eyes of the Piedmontese. All forms of amusement being now over, they spent their time confessing the sins they had committed during Carnival, which were so numerous that the priests were supposed to absolve them 'by the lump'. William in his quiet way was more sociable than the somewhat flashy Lord Carlisle, who declared that the Carnival being over gave him great pleasure, as he was tired to death of going to the opera every night.

> As for the dancing, I am very easy about it, as I can't say I am a great lover of dancing. We finished our carnival with a masquerade ball, where there was a great crowd, and some good masks. I stayed there till the last. This town will seem very dull for some time, as there is a sudden change from being gay, to very stupid. I'll vouch for myself, for I am as stupid as a post this day, and should not undertake writing to you, were it not my resolution of writing to you on the Tuesday, while I remain at Turin.
>
> I imagine, by Emily's last letter, you propose that I should stay some time longer at Turin. All that I wish is to be at Venice at the Ascension, which is in May. By which means I shall have it in my power to bathe in the sea, as either that or Barèges must be thought of in the course of the summer, as I can assure you it is very necessary, and what ought not to be neglected. Them two places I mentioned in a former letter generally swarm with English, by what I hear.

William's next letter from home brought him further news of his brother Charles' new tutor, Mr Ogilvie, who, it will be recalled, was ultimately to become the Duchess of Leinster's second husband. At this time he was just the new tutor, whom William hoped would prove a success:

> February 24th, 1768 ... I wish you joy of Mr Ogilivie's arrival; I hope Charles likes him. I make no doubt but Charles will profit very much. I never mention to you what a much more delightful boy Charles is than Harry Fox, who is humoursome beyond expression; and, what is

still worse, is that they encourage him. Lady Holland is not so bad as Lord Holland and Charles [Fox]; the latter is the worst of any of them in regard to coaxing him. It is a great pity, as he does not want understanding; if everything does not go his own way he cries and pouts for half an hour.

Lord Charles FitzGerald and Harry Fox were about the same age; being eleven-and-a-half and thirteen years old respectively. The former later entered the Royal Navy, rising to the rank of Rear-admiral; he became a Member of the Irish House of Commons; in 1800 he was created Baron Lecale after having voted for the Union. Harry Fox was the fourth,[*] and youngest, son of Lord Holland; when he was fifteen he went into the Army, and became a General in 1808. Unlike his two elder brothers, he did not develop a passion for gambling; Walpole described him as the Hollands' 'only good son'. In his excessive indulgence of Harry, Lord Holland was only pursuing the method of education he had already established for his two elder sons. 'Let nothing be done to break his spirit,' Lord Holland had said of Charles when he was a boy; 'the world will effect that business soon enough.' And in an effort to preserve his sons' spirits he had, as far as was humanly possible, granted them their every wish from the first moment when, lying in their cradles, they were able to make their first wishes known.

> Lord Carlisle is still here. His ribbon is arrived,[**] but he has not yet got it as there is a fuss made about an oath that he is to take, which the King cannot administer as it is to defend our religion; but I imagine they can dispense of it, and that he'll receive it this week.

On 27 February the King of Sardinia invested Lord Carlisle with the Order of the Thistle. The ceremony was performed in the morning in the King's Cabinet; the Royal family and all the prinicipal officers of the court being present.

> The conversation of this town is much changed, as during the carnival it was about musick, singing, dancing, etc., etc. Now it is in which church there was the best sermon. Our winter is near at an end. One begins to see the earth, as we have been in snow these two months past.

---

* Lord Holland's second son, Henry Charles, had died an infant.
** 'I like the badge very well,' wrote the young earl. 'It would have been prettier had it been a little less; but, as it is, I am very well satisfied with it.'

I have quite got the better of my pain in my side, and continue my exercises. I dance every day, and propose being a great minuet dancer. As for country dances, I am very near as lazy as the Dublin gentlemen. But when I see the fair ones in distress for partners I take compassion on them and make a bold effort.

About this time occurred a tragedy in William's household. His servant shot himself. From a brief reference* in an undated (later) letter, it is possible to deduce that William informed his parents of the occurence in a letter that has not survived; for the date of the next letter after one of 24 February quoted above is 9 March – a gap of some thirteen days; and William was, as we know, in the habit of writing to his mother generally about once a week. But we have a description of the tragedy from the pen of William's friend, Lord Carlisle, in a letter he wrote to George Selwyn:

TURIN, March 2, 1768. My dear George, Many thanks for your long letter, which I received the day before yesterday. I paid a visit to-day, as proxy for you,** so I expect you will repay me. Mine was to one** deprived of life; yours shall be to one*** whose health, youth, and beauty, has had more power upon me than ever the most wan ghastly corpse has had over you. A servant of Lord Kildare – the most quiet, sober creature that ever I saw, who has lived with him some years as a footman, and served him with great fidelity – was this morning found shot in his bed. What puzzled us very much was that there were found in his body two wounds, plainly those of pistol-balls. In the room there were found three pistols loaded, and but one discharged; yet, by a paper found in his pocket, we have no reason to doubt but that he was the author of his own death, as he in that paper declares his intentions, and his reasons for so doing, which plainly shows that he has been some time wrong in his head, as his inquietudes of mind are something about walking upon his knees up some steps at Rome, which this poor wretch's madness had taken hold of. He was a most shocking spectacle. What was extraordinary, in the fit of frenzy that he must have been in, was that he should have the coolness to charge the same pistol again, before he could rid himself of that life which, with all our inquiries, seems to have been, or ought to have been, so comfortable to him. He

* 'I was obliged to draw for more on account of my poor servant's wages that are due to him, which I am to remit to his relations.'
** A reference to Selwyn's propensity for viewing corpses.
*** Lady Sarah Bunbury.

enjoyed his master's good opinion; lived well with the other servants, and was, independently of Lord Kildare, in good circumstances. I cannot help dwelling upon this subject, for the sight of him was so horrible that it affected him so very much. He was also a great favourite of mine, as he attended my old friend, poor Ophaly,* during his long illness, with the greatest marks not only of attention, but also affection, and expressed a sorrow at his death, that made me always look upon him as a protégé of mine. I dare say Lady Sarah will be very sorry when she hears of it.

Like other Italian cities, nearly all of which were unlit at night, Turin had its share of lawlessness. 'We had another murder committed near our door the other night,' writes Lord Carlisle. 'None of our servants will walk about the house after sunset but in pairs; they look like the beasts going into Noah's ark.'

William's travels were constantly threatened with interruption on account of events in Ireland. In February of this year (1768) was enacted the Octennial Bill, which provided for a general election every eight years. Formerly the parliament had lasted for a whole reign; and the passing of this measure was the first considerable triumph for the reform movement in Irish constitutional politics, which owed much to the efforts of William's father, the Duke of Leinster, as well as to public opinion generally. Thereafter the Irish Parliament was to be more expressive of the general will. The Octennial Act resulted in Parliament being dissolved the following May. At the General Election in July William was elected unopposed for the Borough of Kildare and also for the City of Dublin; he chose to sit for the latter. He remained a Member of Parliament until his accession to the Dukedom in 1773.

> March the 9th, 1768. My dearest Mother ... The post before I received your obliging letter I received one dated the 11th of February from the Duke, which I answered the next day, being the 5th of this month. In his letter he mentions the necessity he believes I am under of returning home on account of the election. I could wish it was for a better occasion, though I hear we shall have no opposition. I own I shall be very happy at seeing you, though I could have wished to have finished my

---

* George, Earl of Ophaly, William's elder brother, had died in 1765. He had been an Eton friend of Lord Carlisle, who had celebrated him in his *Verses on his Schoolfellows at Eton*.

travels at once, as I should like to settle.

Later he writes: 'I read in our last newspapers of the Duke's being carried home upon the people's shoulders.'

> Our winter (continued William on 9 March) is begun again, as from fine warm weather it is grown quite cold. But all the comfort is that it won't last. I have no great reason to complain as I am hardly ever cold, and my rooms are so cold, that when Lord Carlisle comes in my room he is obliged to put more wood on the fire.

And, later:

> We have had very cold weather, but I believe the spring is now begun, as one sits with the windows open, and one gets a little riding and walking. But the people of the country do not reckon it safe, as they say this is the time of the year for to get a *coup de soleil.*

Lord Carlisle had his dog with him: 'Rover is now sitting in the balcony, barking like a cur at all the coaches. He always goes with me to the promenade with a great brickbat in his mouth.'

William heard often from Lady Holland, who was still at Nice with her husband and two sons. The youngest, Harry, should have been at Eton at this time, but the fond father could not bear to part with him. And the presence of the erudite Charles, he considered, would make up to Harry for anything he might miss by his absence from school. 'Harry,' wrote Lord Holland, 'will lose no learning by being with Charles instead of being at Eton. I am sure I am a great gainer by the latter's kind and cheerful stay here, and if I were to go expatiating upon his and Lord Carlisle's merits, I should never have done. They have, and promise, every agreeable and good quality you can see or foresee in them; and will not either despise themselves, nor be despised by other people, at least these forty years.' The Hollands intended to leave Nice for home at the beginning of April, taking Harry with them, and making 'a great tour' through Switzerland and northern France. Lord Holland's stay at Nice greatly benefited his health – a fact which, according to Sir Horace Mann, did much to create the reputation of Nice – then only a small fishing port – as a salubrious watering-place. Charles was to leave Nice at the same time, and to go by sea to Genoa. Here William and Lord Carlisle proposed to join him; after which William intended returning to Turin, while Charles and Lord Carlisle were to travel south.

7

GENOA – TURIN

On a Saturday morning early in April William and Lord Carlisle, the latter having taken his *congé* of all the royal family, set out from Turin for Genoa. They arrived at Genoa on Sunday about nine o'clock. They found the roads fairly good. They were impressed with the beauty of the Apennines, which were covered with a great quantity of timber, and the cottages scattered in the most romantic situations in a very delightful manner. The wild vegetation seemed in the greatest vigour, and some weeks more forward than in the country they had left. A little botanical knowledge, they agreed, would have made the journey more agreeable. Although the road was one frequented by robbers, they arrived unmolested at their destination.

Genoa the Superb – so-called because of its fine situation and its many palaces – was still the capital of a republic, and still had a Doge as its ruler. It possessed two of the most famous streets in Europe; most of the others were too narrow for coaches. Trade and banking had brought great riches to the nobles; but, like other Italian cities, the streets were dirty and filled with beggars. The palaces were noble, and filled with fine pictures; with the use of painted perspective, looking 'more like scenery than real houses'. Along the main street was a row of palaces on each side, faced with marble, and of excellent architecture. Among the princely families the most celebrated were the Dorias. In the sixteenth century Andrea Doria imposed on the republic the architect Alessi, to whom most of the palaces along the principal street owe their creation. Besides the palaces, Genoa boasted many medieval churches; the dominating cathedral of San Lorenzo; and the house of Christopher Columbus.

William stayed in Genoa only a few days, and then, saying goodbye to Lord Carlisle, hurried back to Turin, missing Charles Fox who, on his way to Genoa by sea from Nice, was delayed by bad weather, for the rains had set in, and the felucca men would never go to sea at the least sign of bad weather. A French courier arrived with the news that Charles was wind-bound 'in a little miserable place called Noli, about thirty miles distant'. Lord Carlisle, therefore, decided to wait for him'; especially as the weather looked a little clearer. The young earl, having seen everything in the town worth seeing, was now confined in solitude to his room in a wretched inn – 'for I cannot go out without unpacking all my clothes, and that is too much trouble' – amusing himself with his dog Rover, and reading Hume's history and, in Italian, *Davila's History of the Civil Wars in France*.

The day following his return to Turin, William described his impression of Genoa:

> Turin, April the 9th, 1768. I returned last night from Genoa, which had prevented my writing my usual post day. I must give you some idea of Genoa, which is a very curious town to see, but not to stay in, I believe. It is built upon the side of the Apennines. There is a very fine bay and harbour. The town is large, and the buildings fine. The streets are very narrow so that coaches cannot pass. There are but two streets broad enough for carriages, and them two streets are very fine, as there are some of the most beautiful palazzi in Italy, well furnished with fine pictures of all the old masters. The weather was so bad that we could not go out to sea for to see the view of the town. I was in hopes to have seen Charles Fox, but he was prevented by the badness of the weather.
>
> You would oblige me by sending me word in what manner you would have me finish my tour of Italy. The summer is a bad time of year for going to Vienna, as everybody is in the country, as I am informed by a letter I received from Vienna; but whatever the Duke or you settle will be agreeable to me, as it is quite the same thing where I go, as I find I amuse myself everywhere. ... I can assure you I study economy very much, as I am very sensible of the lowness of the Duke's stock. The last quarter was less than the former and I make no doubt but I shall reduce this if I stay here. I am willing to delay Venice till the latter end of summer, as by all accounts it is very disagreeable in the hot weather, which is just the time that I intended being there, and my being so well, that I should think one might delay the sea bathing till September; and from thence to Vienna.
>
> April the 16th, 1768 ... I hope you received my letter of the 9th instant, wherein I mention some intentions in regard to my proceedings; I am afraid you'll think me changeable. I am at present in a very regular way of business with my masters, which employ me from 8 in the morning till 1 o'clock. I mentioned to you in my last my not going to the

Ascension. With your permission I propose staying here till the great heats come; then, with your leave, I shall go to Milan, which is reckoned the coolest town in Italy; and afterwards proceed to Parma, etc., etc.; and from thence to Venice, where I propose bathing. I have several letters from Milan, especially one from Lady Holland to Count Fimian,[*] who is a prodigious good kind of a sensible man, a man by all accounts worthy of being acquainted with. As to Vienna, till the latter end autumn is a bad season, especially as the Emperor makes the tour of his dominions this summer. I am afraid, but I can assure you I have not, and shall like spending my winter there very much.

Bolle ... has nothing particular to say except my being in a very good state of health. (The fleas begin to bite terrible; I only killed 2 yesterday.)

The King of Sardinia's birthday was on 27 April, and in the morning William went to Court.

April 27th, 1768 ... Our weather is very pleasant, but the sun is too hot. The country is beautiful, as the trees are coming out. There is a great want of rain, but I dread its coming as it never ends when once it comes. The evenings are pleasant enough. The ladies go out airing every evening. The Sundays and holidays the promenade is very agreeable, as all the fine ladies are in their coaches, and the beautiful bourgeois afoot.

I have thoughts of going to Milan during the great heats, which must be insupportable here, as we are so environed with mountains.

The Duke of Devonshire is expected every day; I hear he is prodigious silent young man.

William Cavendish, 5th Duke of Devonshire, had succeeded his father in 1764. He was a year older than William, and lived until 1811.

4th of May, 1768 ... The Duke of Devonshire left this yesterday; he is a very bashful young man, speaks very little and is *bien sauvage et bien gauche*. He returns soon. At present I am left almost alone, except just one or two that are at the Academy.

We have had a great deal of rain these two [days] past, which will bring on the hot weather soon. At present it seems to be clearing up ...

I approve much of your scheme of finishing my travels at once, and if Miss FitzGerald and I can agree, I should look upon myself as the happiest of beings. But I am afraid the chance is but small, as I hear the Kingstons are determined to have her. Lady Holland approves very

---

* Governor of Milan.

much of the match, and, I believe, has wrote to you about it, as I used to talk seriously about it. She proposes being in England the 23rd of this month. I have the pleasure of hearing very often from her.

14th of May, 1768. My dearest Mother, I did not write last post knowing that Bolle writ, and that I had nothing particular to say. I can with pleasure assure you that I am very much better than when he wrote last. I lead a very regular life which I find agrees very well with me. I make but two meals a day, which is breakfast and dinner. The former is nothing but strawberries and bread, and the dinner is very slight. I find that eating so much is a very foolish vanity, as eating little answers the same purpose.

I go on the same as usual, and amuse myself very well. The weather has been very pleasant and the drives about here are delightful. The Court goes to the country next week, as does also a great deal of the nobility. I have been invited by many to come and spend a few days with them, which I propose doing, by way of seeing their way of living in the country. But I have no great opinion of their society. The worst is the heat will oblige one to stay at home a good deal. I believe I shall often think how much pleasanter we live at Carton. Pray, what do you propose that I should do when I remove from this? I suppose you still continue your intention of my spending my winter at Vienna. I propose taking a good deal of sea bathing in the autumn at Venice. I should like to stay a few weeks at Milan and Parma.

My dancing master has been of great service to me, as it is amazing how much wider I am upon the chest; all my waistcoats are too tight. My legs also are fine; in short, I believe I shall return a fine genteel figure! I do not grow fat, which is a comfort.

Pray, my love to the Duke, and tell him that the news that is the great talk of this town at present is that the Genoese have given up the towns in Corsica that remained in their hands to the French, and that the French are certainly going to send ten thousand men there. But what they are to do when they get there is not yet known. I saw a letter from Paoli the other day that mentions it, wherein he seems to be alarmed at it.

Pasquale Paoli, the famous Corsican general and patriot, was head of the Corsican government from 1757 to 1768. He had driven the Genoese* from the whole island except a few coast towns. During this month (May, 1768) Genoa, unable to subdue the Corsicans under

* In February, 1768, the Genoese forbade the Corsicans at Genoa to wear any swords, whereupon Paoli ordered all the Genoese in Corsica to wear two!
                                    – Earl of Carlisle to Selwyn, 20 Feb, 1768

Paoli, sold Corsica to France. It was during this same year that Boswell's *Account of Corsica, with Memoirs of General Paoli* was published; the following year appeared his *Essays in Favour of the Brave Corsicans*. In spite of his early successes, and of his exertions to maintain the independence of his native country against the Genoese and French, Paoli was in the end compelled to yield to the overwhelming military power of France, and to seek safety in flight. Having made his way to the sea coast, he embarked, on 16 June, 1769, on board an English vessel, in which he proceeded, in the first instance, to Leghorn, and afterwards crossed the continent to England. In this country, where he subsequently passed nearly 40 years, he was received with every token of admiration and respect. He died at his residence in Edgware Road in 1807.

> The other news, (continued William on 14 May) altho' not formed upon so good authority, is that the King of Prussia proposes coming into Switzerland with fourteen thousand men to subdue the people of Neuchatel, who have killed his Governor.

> May 21st, 1768 ... You must excuse the shortness of this letter, as the French ambassador has sent to me just now to come dine with him, and I have hardly time to dress. He is the civilest young man I ever met with. I dine there very often, and [he] says I do not come often enough. His wife is a good kind of a woman.

The French Ambassador to Turin and his wife were both very popular, civil and well-bred. Many Englishmen enjoyed their hospitality, and found it a pleasure to talk to them; for the French of the Piedmontese was not the most pure. The ambassador was a member of the Choiseul family. He and the ambassadress frequently invited William to their house; it was, indeed, the house he frequented the most; he dined there almost twice a week.

William found it very necessary to continue with his Italian master, for he had 'little or no practice, as everybody speaks French here'. He was fond of his studies: 'I continue spending my time very agreeably and continue my masters; mathematicks and dancing masters are very great favourites.'

It was now the end of May, and William began to suffer from the heat. To add to his discomfort, he was 'obliged to wear black clothes as the Court is in mourning for one of the Duke of Savoy's children'. The hot weather compelled him to give up his fencing master. The hot weather also brought out the flies:

> June the 1st, 1768 ... You would laugh to see the figure I am at present,
> with a great black patch across my face, as I cut myself in a most bar-
> barous manner as I was shaving myself yesterday. I must own it was a
> very awkward manoeuvre, but it'll make me more careful another time.
> It was not quite so much my fault, as a fly kept buzzing about my ear.
>   Our weather still continues pleasant, as we have had a little rain,
> which has refreshed the air. In about a week I propose going into the
> country. I am invited to go to another person's house in July.

By the end of this month – June – William would have been almost
two years abroad. He and Mr Bolle now made their annual examina-
tion of their accounts; which they found came to 'an enormous sum'.
The masters had run away with a great sum, especially the dancing
master. 'I believe,' wrote William, 'if you was to see me dance you
would say the money was not lost'. In spite of the large amounts they
had drawn – a large number of William's letters throughout his
Grand Tour end with the postscript 'I have been obliged to draw for
money' – they were still short.

> 8th of June, 1768 ... I am sorry that I am now obliged to touch upon
> money matters. But as the end of this month finishes our year, I shall
> be obliged to raise the sum, I am afraid; as I intend clearing everything
> and pay my masters and all bills, and begin the year fresh with the hopes
> of reducing the yearly sum, as I flatter myself I have done this year. As
> for clothes, I am very well off. I shall escape summer clothes again this
> year, as we are at present in mourning and likely to continue. And
> besides our own Court mourning, and we have one here, which lasts
> the summer, and are likely to have one for the Queen of France. As for
> winter clothes, I am very well off in case I spend my winter at Vienna.

Marie Leszczynska, daughter of Stanislas Leszczynski, King of
Poland, and wife of Louis XV, died at Versailles on 24 June 1768.
    William was now able to give his mother a clearer idea of his
plans for the latter part of the summer, and for the winter:

> June the 15th, 1768. I was made very happy by your obliging letter of
> the 16th of May, and am very glad you approve of my going to Milan.
> But I do not propose going till the beginning of August, as next month
> I propose going into the country, as I mentioned to you in some for-
> mer letters; and afterwards to Milan, and so finish my tour of Italy and

take a good deal of sea bathing at Venice, and so on to Vienna.

I am not entered at the Academy, but have all the masters but the riding, which is no great loss, as it is fallen off of late. There are some little inconveniences in regard to entering, that as you left it to me, I thought best not to enter.

I do not propose making any long stay anywhere else in Italy, as there is nothing very tempting, and I would choose to be at Vienna before the winter comes on, as it is very bad winter travelling. I make no doubt but I shall spend my time well there. I make no doubt but that I shall be well received, as there are so many Irish officers who are great men there. When I get to Germany I shall begin to think that I am approaching home, which I own will be a comfort, as the time appears long. But as you say, it is for my improvement, which it is certainly, as well as for many other reasons.

The Duke of Devonshire is expected here soon. I certainly shall try what I can to get acquainted with him, silent as he is. I can't say I miss Lord Carlisle, as he is certainly a great coxcomb; and what is worse is that [he] despises everybody, especially foreigners. He would not allow there was a sensible person here, which is a thing he could not judge of, as he never opened his lips to any of them. And they say here, *qu'il portez un aire d'ennuye partous ou il y allez.* They were inclined to be very civil to him, but he never would go near any of them. If he did he never finished ten minutes in any assembly he went to. The ladies were very much inclined to be in love with him, which I do not wonder at, as he is certainly a pretty man and his green ribbon became him much.

Carlisle's letters to Selwyn at this time seem to show that William's judgement of the young man was fair. It will be recalled that the opera, the social centre of the city, had bored the earl 'to death'. His opinion of the male society had been low. 'The Piedmont men,' he declared, 'are as stupid as Frenchmen'. He thought a little better of the women, but only because they were young. 'Since I have been at Turin,' he had said, 'I have not been in company with two old women. In Paris, as you know, every room is filled with that lumber.'

You are desirous of knowing the people I am acquainted with; it would take up a sheet of paper as there is hardly anybody that I do not know. But them I frequent the most, are Madame Vorghera, who has three fine daughters, and she lives quite in a family way; Madame St Gilles; Madame d'Aglié, who is married to the King's favourite; Madame Bourgaretti, who is the handsomest woman here and a *belle esprit.* Them are the Piedmontese that I frequent the most, besides many men;

also the foreign ministers, especially the French ambassador, who is the politest little man in the world.

William mixed not only with the Italian families living at Turin, but also with many young Englishmen who were, as he himself was, making the Grand Tour. He was always glad to see Charles Fox, who now arrived in the city on his way to Switzerland.

> July the 13th, 1768 ... Lord Fitzwilliam, Mr Charles Fox, and a Mr Price arrived here yesterday, but they propose going in a few days. We are about ten English at present, and eight of us were at Eton together. It is amazing how one picks up our old Eton acquaintances abroad. I dare say I have met above forty since I have been in Italy.

Uvedale Price, a young man of 21, had, like FitzWilliam and Fox, been at Eton with William. He now accompanied Charles Fox into Switzerland; together the following month, August, they visited Voltaire at Ferney. The sage was by now a very old man, so that the visit could be but a short one. He led the young men into his garden, and talked with them there, walking backwards and forwards. He gave them some chocolate, and a list of his books to read, and then said good bye.

William's popularity at Court was such that enquiries were made as to the possibility of his succeeding George Pitt, whose appointment ended that year, as Envoy. It will be recalled that Pitt had been appointed in 1761; after spending only two years in Turin, he went on leave in 1764 and did not return. He had, therefore, been absent from his post for a period of four years.

> 31st of July, 1768 ... You'll be surprised at what I am going to write, as well as I was when I heard it. You must know, that it seems Mr. Pitt does not return here; and as our Chargé des Affaires was talking with the Secretary of State, who flung out a hint that the Court here would be very happy in having me. Upon which the Chargé des Affaires said I was so young; he said that was nothing to the purpose. To be sure, it was a greater honour than I merited from the Court, who, to be sure, on all occasions have shewn great attention to me, and commended me much for my *sagesse* (to be sure, I am not a little proud of it). I was advised to mention it to you to know whether the Duke of Leinster thought it a proper thing for me. I hope you will not think it an idea of mine, as I never thought of it till it was mentioned to me. In the first

place, I look upon myself as a great deal too young to enter into public affairs; in the next place, I own I long to get back, and see whether it'll be possible to succeed with the certain Miss if the Duke of Leinster and you approved of the match.

I hope you'll not be displeased in my having mentioned this, and I beg the Duke of Leinster will act just as he thinks proper, as whatever he does and chooses me to do is always what will please me, as I look upon him to be the proper judge and think myself in duty bound to be at his disposal; as I am sure no son has reason to be more content or happier than me, as, to be sure, both yours and his goodness to me is beyond expression. And I hope, when I return, you'll be content with me, as I am sure I do everything in my power to make myself a dutiful son; and I fancy my time has not been lost by travelling; I own I find a great advantage in it.

William was not, however, appointed Envoy to the Court of Turin.

After the hot weather of May came the rains of June. Towards the end of June the rain stopped, the sun came out, and there was 'no stirring out till 6 or 7 o'clock in the evening'. The heat became so intense that William gave up his dancing lessons for the time being. He sat in his room behind closed shutters, trying to keep cool.

You must excuse if this letter is not of my best writing, [he wrote in July] as I am obliged to write almost in the dark, as by shutting out the light is the only way to keep the room cool; so I shut the window and shutters curtain besides the *penden-d'aire*, which is by way of keeping out the sun. So you may imagine I am enough in the dark; if it were not for the doors, which you leave open, we should have no air.

The great heat continued throughout July and August, with intermittent rain. 'Altogether,' wrote William towards the end of July, 'this is a very disagreeable summer climate, as the weather is very changeable; the mountains being so near that they draw the clouds, which occasions a very suffocating heat'. And, a month later: 'the weather has been most amazingly hot, which indeed continues, tho' we have had rain, which they said would have carried off the heat; but instead of carrying it off, in my opinion, it has increased it.'

To add to his physical discomfort, William was eaten up by fleas:

One of the greatest happinesses I shall have in returning will be to get rid of the fleas, etc. I may very well say, as Captain Macheath does, that one at a time is enough for most mortals to bear, but two at a time no mortal can bear; at least, two fleas are not bearable, which I have had just now and at present have a third. What would poor Emily do if she was in my case? ... I have them by the dozen, and killed about a third part, so you may imagine there is left sufficient number to eat me up; I eat, drink and sleep well, when the fleas will permit; Among the many other misfortunes in the course of my travels I have at last got to be as lousy as a person can well be; but I am now in hopes that I have got quite rid of them, as I have had fifty killed, and have filled my head with Spanish snuff, which is a sure cure.

In spite of the heat and the fleas, William had not forgotten Miss FitzGerald; throughout the summer months his letters are peppered with references to the young woman:

Your accounts of Miss FitzGerald are very good. I think it'll be delightful. She'll be just of a proper age by the time I go back, if not disposed of before, as I am very much afraid of the Kingstons; ... When you mention Miss FitzGerald in your last I hope you was serious; ... Pray, is Miss FitzGerald to make you a visit this year?; ... If we could but make ourselves sure of Miss FitzGerald, we shall be very happy and content. But I can't say I flatter myself too much, for fear of disappointment. I hope she is to make you a visit at Carton this summer; ... I am glad to find by Emily's letter that you have had such good company at Carton; amongst others Miss FitzGerald, who you all seem to like. Emily does give a very good account of her, but I do not find you are sure of having her at Carton for to stay, which would be a delightful way of getting thoroughly acquainted with her.

Among the purchases that William made during his Italian tour was, as has been mentioned, a set of books of Etruscan vases, printed by subscription at Naples under the direction of the British Envoy, William Hamilton. William subscribed for his father, and also for his aunt, Lady Louisa Connolly, and had them sent, as they appeared, to London. At the beginning of the summer of 1768 he wrote to his family to let them know of the safe arrival of the first volume:

Lady Louisa's quick return must have been very agreeable to you. I wrote to her some time ago, but I am afraid my letter did not arrive till after she had left London. It was partly to acquaint her that her first book of Etruscan vases was to be had at Mr George Ross, agent, in Conduit Street, where, if you are impatient for ours, you'll be so kind as to write to somebody in London to send it you; you must ask for it in my name, as I believe it was my name that is put to the subscription.

Most likely by the time you get this there will be another volume ready.

From Turin he sent other presents:

> As to your sugar plums, I am trying to get some here, as I have a very
> good opportunity of sending them to England. If they are not good and
> I thought you could wait, I would write to Naples, for that is the
> famous place for them, especially Diavolonis, but I am informed that I
> can get them here. I shall make a very strict enquiry.

By July he was getting anxious to know whether his Roman carnations had arrived:

> Pray, are the carnations safe or not? Here there are a great profusion of
> them, but no very fine double ones. The colours are beautiful, especial-
> ly the straw-coloured ones. But they are small. Your sugar plums are
> bespoke. I propose sending them by sea in a case with a few books that
> I want to send to Ireland, which I have read, and are curious, and that
> are very inconvenient to carry about.

During August the previous year (1767) William, when in Florence,
had ordered some vases to be made and sent to his mother. It was,
therefore, with dismay that he now heard that they had arrived in
Ireland – broken:

> You cannot imagine how sorry as well as surprised [I was to hear] of the
> melancholy accident of the Etruscan vases; but am glad to find they are
> so well mended and to your liking. To be sure, it is a pity they are
> broke, as, to be sure, they are an honour to my good taste. If I had
> remained at Florence to have seen them packed up, I should have flat-
> tered myself to have taken more care of them in the packing. The first
> letter that I write to Florence shall be to scold the man who sent them,
> as he promised me to pack them up safe.

As we have seen, it was William's intention to go to Milan; then to
Venice for the sea-bathing; and afterwards to Vienna, where he
hoped to arrive in November, before the winter set in. He had spent
the greater part of a year in Turin, and during that time he had
come to know a large number of people: 'I shall be rather sorry to
leave Turin, as I have so many acquaintances here; I do not know
how I shall manage to leave all my acquaintances here, for I have so
many. I may venture to say I have more acquaintances here than I
have in London.'

William was looking forward to the long journey from Turin to Vienna. He now had the prospect of covering the distance in fair weather; he no longer had the apprehension he had felt the previous year when the winter had already begun and he would have had to encounter snow-bound roads:

> I have just this minute been talking about Vienna with a gentleman that has been there; he advises me to be there early in November. I make no doubt but that I shall spend my time very well there. I am told it is prodigiously cold, which will brace my nerves; after the warm climate of Italy, it'll be good as a cold bath. I have lately seen a gentleman who is just arrived from Vienna and gives me a delightful account of it. I hope to set off very soon. I shall make a very short stay at Milan, as almost everybody is in the country. I propose going directly to Count Firmian, who Lady Holland has given me a letter to; and he has sent to me to come to his country seat, as he'll be very glad to see me. By all accounts he is a most amiable, agreeable man. I have picked up many letters for Vienna.

As the time drew near for their departure from Turin, Mr Bolle became happier. It was not that he was unhappy with his young master – far from it. But Mr Bolle had left a wife at home, and he had been away from her for more than two years. No pleasures encountered while making the Grand Tour could make up for his being absent from her. Bolle 'continues very well,' wrote William, 'and longs to get home to see his dear, who I believe is also very impatient'. And at the beginning of August Bolle 'is very busy arranging my clothes for the journey. For the good man must have his time to prepare for a journey, especially as he means packing up winter coats and not to disturb them till we arrive at Vienna, which I hope will be early in November.' Every day brought him one day nearer to reunion with his wife. He was 'not sorry to leave Italy'.

William had lately been troubled with a 'humour' in his feet!

> My feet [he wrote in August] are very troublesome, especially as I am deprived of one of the greatest amusements of this town, which is walking at Citadel and about the streets at night; which is very gay, as there is all the world and musick, as serenading is much the fashion in this country. I propose leaving this place as soon as my feet will permit, and I am now in hopes that the hot weather is almost over, especially as now seems set in to rain.

And, later the same month,

It is with great pleasure I can assure you of my feet being almost well, and I hope in a very few days to be ready to set off for Vienna, for where I have already picked up a great many letters to and from different people. So I make no doubt but that I shall spend my time very well ... We are at present a great number of Englishmen, but most of them going into Italy. I imagine Vienna will be a good place, as very few English make any stay there. I own I shall feel rather sorry at leaving this. I propose going into the country this week, and afterwards to Count Massin's, who is the most gentlemanlike man here, and lives on the road to Milan. He has made me promise to call on him in my way there.

William's last letter from Turin was written early in September, just before his departure to the country:

7th of September, 1768. Carissima mia Madre, I begin by apologising for the shortness of this letter, being just on the brink of setting out for the country, where I stay two days, and then I propose setting out immediately for Milan. I own I am rather impatient to get to Venice, as your letters are all addressed there ... I can with pleasure assure you of my being in perfect health, and better than I have been for some time, especially since the hot weather has left us. Bolle has got very well again, which I own I am glad of as I was rather uneasy; but he is in very good spirits. I fancy this will be the last letter you'll receive from Turin; and, indeed, I am almost ashamed to send this, being so short, but I hope you'll excuse it, as it is only to keep up my rule of not missing writing once a week to you, and as Bolle does not write.

And so, after a stay of nearly eleven months in Turin, William and Bolle once again stepped into their carriage and set out on a further stage of their travels. Looking out through the narrow carriage windows they saw for the last time those tree-lined streets, the arcaded squares and the elegant palaces which they had come to know so well. Between the houses they caught glimpses of the Alps. The postillion urged the horses into a fast trot. Behind the box sat a servant. The luggage which Bolle had so carefully packed with William's clothes was safely stowed away. The carriage rattled and jolted through the streets. It was 'but a small town'; soon the last house was passed. Now they looked out on the autumnal countryside and the grand mountains which partly encircle the city.

8

MILAN – VENICE

On leaving Turin William went to stay in the country; first, with the Marquis d'Aglié, and secondly, with Count Massin. Afterwards he continued on his way to Milan. The journey from Turin to Milan could be made in comfort. The roads were good. The borders of Piedmont were as yet unclaimed, and consisted of waste marshland. Passing over the gentle river Ticino, William came into the rich land of Lombardy. The mulberry trees were beginning to turn to autumn colours. Dark grapes hung from the vines which festooned the mulberry trees. Great red pumpkins lay along the ground beneath them.

William's regret at leaving Turin was not lessened by his early impressions of Milan. His first letter from the city recalls the friendliness of the Sardinian Court, and describes the hospitality he had received during his country visits:

> Milan, the 17th September, 1768. I write these few lines to acquaint you of my having left Turin and being arrived safe at Milan. I can assure you that I felt very sorry when the day came, especially when I took leave of my friends. From the King down to the last of his subjects that I was acquainted with overcame me with civilities. The Duke of Savoy and the Duchess were remarkably gracious. In short, I did not think it in the power of people to be so civil.
>
> In my last from Turin I mentioned I was just a going into the country. I was at the Marquis d'Aglié and afterwards at Count Massin. Both places I received the greatest civilities; which a course made me spend my time very agreeably. I suppose you will like to know their way of living in the country. The morning one gets up and breakfasts in our own rooms and afterwards we generally took a walk, and then returned and played at cards till dinner. After dinner cards till evening, then we went a walking. After that we retired into a little room on the ground floor which is called the coffee house *á l'anglois*, where we drunk coffee and stayed till we went upstairs to play.

The houses are very agreeable and pleasant; they have generally a large gallery, where they sit in, which is comfortable. The Marquis D'Aglié is a very good old house with a pretty garden, but the situation is low and flat. They have a little ditch which they call a canal (in the English taste) but altogether it was very agreeable, except rather too much of cards. I hope you'll excuse the shortness of this, as I am going to be presented to the Duke of Modena who holds his Court here. I shall in my next give you an account of him as well as of Count Massin's country seat, which is beautiful.

24th September. In my last I promised to give you an account of the Count of Massin's beautiful situated country house. It is situated upon a ridge of hills almost in the middle of a plain surrounded by hills, which is prodigious well cultivated, and watered by a charming serpentine river that comes running from the Alps, which are at a very pleasant distance. Besides the river there are two small lakes, which one sees from the house, which is an old one but rendered very comfortable, and made very agreeable by the civilities of the master, who is as gentlemanlike a man as ever I met with, and one who has seen a great deal of the world.

I have been presented here to the Duke of Modena, who is upwards of sixty years of age, and wears a wig with about 100 curls, and wears rouge, and adorns his forehead with white.

A few years earlier Francis III d'Este, Duke of Modena, (1698-1780) had married, as his second wife, the Countess Simonetti, an old woman as painted as himself. Horace Walpole said of them, 'Their faces must run together like a palette of colours'.

Since my arrival at Milan, I have been a good deal hurried in seeing things, though the town is horrid ugly, yet there is some few things to see, in and about it.

The city, had indeed, no such attraction for English travellers as had Rome or Naples. Four days were considered enough in which to see the sights. The people, however, were very hospitable, especially towards Englishmen, for those who stayed longer than a few days there were assemblies and balls. As for the Scala, ten more years were to elapse before its completion in 1778. The streets were lively enough; in the evenings they were filled with fashionable ladies and gentlemen parading in their carriages, passing and repassing in the great piazza about the cathedral.

Milan, the third city in Italy for population and wealth, had, owing to its successive subjugation by France, Spain and Austria, acquired a cosmopolitan atmosphere. The Germanic influence was noticeable in the simple honesty of the people; the French in their fondness of pomp and elegance in equipages and household furniture. Under Spanish rule Milan and the surrounding country had been sadly neglected. Debts had been accumulated, trade and agriculture had declined, the people had been impoverished. During the eighteenth century, after Milan came under Austrian domination, reforms of all kinds were instituted. Trade revived; the people grew richer and therefore happier. 'The period of Maria Theresa,' writes Tivaroni, 'in the memory of the Lombards who could compare it with the Spanish, remained the age of gold.'

Soon after his arrival in Milan William went to see Lake Maggiore; and in his letter of 24 September he describes his visit:

Sir Watkin Williams-Wynne and a Mr Hamilton (who is here at present) we made a jaunt to the Lago Maggiore, which, to be sure, is beyond description. It is the largest lake I ever saw, and the banks about it are beautifully disposed; one sees the prettiest natural cascades come tumbling down thro' the woods and vines, and the banks prodigious well cultivated from top to bottom. You have the Alps at a proper distance over the cultivated hills, which have such a majestic look that's mighty pleasing to the eye; it is not in the power of my pen to express the beauties of the lake and its environs. The Borromean Islands which are on the lake disappointed me much, as I expected to have seen the works of nature; instead of it we found the worst of art. To be sure, our jaunt was delightful, as our two days were very favourable. That added to all our conveniences, which we thank Count Firmian for, who spoke to the Count Borromeo, who was so civil as to order this bark to attend us wherever we chose to go, and ordered his house on one of the islands for our reception. We had about fifteen miles to go by water, by going out of our way for to see the different views of the lake at least made eighteen or twenty miles by water.

Count Firmian, who I have mentioned before in my former letters, answers all my expectations. I do think he is a model of a man of the world in his behaviour and character. His civilities, his attention and his affability is charming, accompanied by a very cleared head, a great knowledge of the world as well as of lecture. I think I never knew a man answer so entirely to one's expectation. He is going a party to see another lake and insists on our being of the party, and has delayed my journey of a few days. By all accounts it is more beautiful than the other, which I cannot believe. If so, I doubt I shall find our lakes nothing. We are to stay five or six days with him.

William stayed with Count Firmian on Lake Como; it was not until he arrived in Venice that he found time to write a description of it; but for the sake of unity we quote the passage here:

> Venice, the 12th of October. I promised you in my last to give some account of the Lago di Como, where I went to spend a few days with Count Firmian. The lake is about forty miles in length. The house where we lived at was about the middle. This lake being situated in the mountains makes it very romantic; to be sure, the views are beyond description. This lake one may almost say it makes three lakes. as one does not see the length on account of the mountains projecting into the water. To be sure, we passed our time agreeably enough, as the water was mighty fine, and we were at least seven hours a day upon the water, where we had the pleasure of a great deal of Count Firmian's company, who, to be sure, is one of the most sensible and the most amiable and most agreeable men I ever met with.

William left Milan at the beginning of October. He took the road eastward toward Venice, passing through Verona and Vicenza. Verona, with its surrounding mountains, rushing river, medieval beauty, and fine Roman amphitheatre, appealed most to William. 'I was much pleased with Verona and Vicenza,' he wrote in his letter from Venice of 12 October,

> Verona especially, as there is some noble pieces of antiquity. The amphitheatre is really noble, tho', to be sure, the inside has been repaired. But at the same time it gives you a most just idea of an amphitheatre. They have now made a kind of a stage where they act plays in the open air. I must own my curiosity led me to see a spectacle in so ancient a theatre; they compute to hold about twenty-five thousand people when full, which, to be sure, must be a most noble sight.

William appreciated Vicenza also, with its masterpieces by Palladio – the town hall and the Olympic theatre – and its many fine palaces.

William's carriage rattled on along the road to Venice, through the deserted and grass-grown streets of Padua, and along the banks of the River Brenta, in whose calm waters was reflected Palladio's famous villa Malcontenta.

And so William arrived at Venice.

VENICE, the 12th of October ... I arrived at Venice a few days ago. I can't say much but its being curious to recommend it, as it seems to be the most disagreeable place I ever was in. Especially as I am quite alone and have not a house to go to, as Sir James Wright, who's our Resident here, who is a very agreeable man, and also Lady Wright, who is an agreeable woman, but is and has been so ill ever since I have been here, that one cannot enjoy either his or her good company.

At this time Venice still ranked as one of the most important cities in Italy. It was, however, but a shadow of its former self; the days when it was Queen of the Adriatic and made its power felt in the Far East were now only a tradition. Although glorified by the name of Republic, Venice was in fact ruled by a narrow obligarchy, under which the 'common people' had no importance. In the Public accounts of 1773 military expenses amount to more than a million ducats, but the expenses for education do not appear at all, and those for public works are scarcely hinted at. But it was not only the 'common people' who were excluded from all voice in the government; most of the nobility were also kept out. Power was exercised by a few of the wealthiest families; the rest of the population acquiesced in complete indifference. A tiny army of 4,000 men was responsible for the safety of the Venetian provinces. Three thousand lanterns lighted the city at night. In spite of these precautions, beggars and vagabonds were to be seen in great numbers in the city and the country, and thieves carried on their occupation everywhere with the greatest success.

In many respects the Republic was in a bad way. Everyone was poor. The nobles did nothing useful, and spent their time gaming and whoring. The arts and crafts in which Venice had been preeminent had sadly declined. Glass-making was in great decadence; the manufacture of iron and the working of gold had enormously decreased in quantity and quality. But in spite of all this, the city had lost none of its pride. Traditional jealousy and suspicion prevented the nobles from holding any conversation with ambassadors or foreign ministers. Even to communicate with them through a third person was risky. The life of a foreign minister in Venice was, therefore, extremely dull and unsociable; and the channel through which young gentlemen on their travels would naturally find access to the best company was stopped up. The government employed spies to report on anyone criticising the conduct of state affairs. It was natural therefore, that the Venetian nobility avoided possible trouble by having no unnecessary relations with foreigners. Traditional exclusiveness had in the course of generations hardened into a fixed social custom. Foreigners might meet members of the Venetian nobility at a café or on the Broglio, but were not ordinarily invited to their houses or their social gatherings, and accordingly found less society at Venice than in most of the cities of Italy.

In these circumstances, it is not surprising to find William bored with the life of Venice. Living alone, with the British Resident unable to entertain him on account of Lady Wright's illness, and the doors of the Venetian nobles closed to all foreigners, we can understand why the sociable young Irishman felt solitary and depressed, and took a dislike to the city. The loveliness of the place can by loneliness be turned to melancholy. If William had been in Venice during the Carnival, he would probably have enjoyed himself more. At that time the city was gay with festivities, and crowded with people from all over Europe.

For a few days William's life was brightened by the company of two fellow-Irish, Mr and Mrs King:

[12th of October.] ... There left this the other day a Mr and Mrs King, both Irish, which made those few days agreeable, she being a very agreeable woman; most likely Lady Sarah* must have mentioned her, as she is a friend of hers, as they were at Spa together. At present there is nobody, and the Venetians not receiving strangers makes it still more disagreeable; and if they did they are almost all in the country.

I have begun my sea bathing, which is, to be sure, the only thing that should keep me here at this time of the year. I own I shall be mighty happy to get to Vienna, where I make no doubt but what I shall be before you can answer this here.

19th of October ... I am very glad to find you approve of my scheme for next spring; to be sure, if accomplished it will be very agreeable; but I am afraid I shall not be able to do it, as things seem to be in an odd situation. I have been obliged to leave off the sea bathing for some days past, as I have been with a complaint in my stomach and bowels which I hope has quite left me; and intend beginning the sea bathing again tomorrow; and if I find it does not agree with me, I shall take a little tour upon the terra firma by way of settling myself for the Vienna journey; as here one is quite out of exercise, as the gondola is so indulgent

* Lady Sarah Bunbury, William's aunt.

that I don't know how I shall accustom myself to the carriage. But I hope to continue the bathing at least fourteen nights more and then set out immediately for Vienna, as I am afraid the winter will be coming on very soon and make it disagreeable. I have some pleasure in the thoughts of advancing northwards, as I must own I long very much to get home, as, to be sure, it is a long while since I have had the pleasure of seeing you. I hope you'll excuse the shortness of this letter, but I have been out all this morning with Sir James Wright, our Minister here, seeing of curiosities; and this evening is the first that Lady Wright sees company after her illness. It being the day of writing to you, I would not lose the least moment that I had to spare.

It will be recalled that a little while previous to this, William had written to his mother telling her that the Turin Court was anxious to have him as British Envoy. He now received her opinion on the matter, and he hastened to reply:

28th of October, 1768 ... To be sure, in regard to Turin, I think the Duke of Leinster and you are perfectly right, as it certainly is not a desirable nor had I set my heart on it, as I can assure you it was at the desire of a friend that I mentioned it. Certainly it would be a direct stop to what I have more at heart, which is the thoughts of settling, in the manner you mention. I may venture to say that you have made me very happy in seeming to give in to my intention, and by giving me such good news, in the regard of the little King.

I propose setting out on Monday for Vienna, so you must not be surprised at not hearing from us till we are settled, the which will be at least ten days or a fortnight.

I have taken a little jaunt on terra firma which has set me up a little; as, to be sure, the air of Venice did not agree with me at all, and shall be glad to get out of it. Very good accounts of Vienna from everybody; I make no doubt but that I shall be content with my sejour ...

I do not know whether you are acquainted with Lady Wright, who is recovered from her illness, and I have had the pleasure of seeing her several times. She is one of the most agreeable women I ever met with. To be sure, after living with foreign ladies, seeing one of our own nation is a comfort, and gives one room to see how far superior our English ladies are to foreign ones in regard to their behaviour and manners.

Bolle is, thank God, mighty well and very happy to get out of Italy; and I may venture to say that nothing will persuade him to return. Mrs Bolle is very impatient for his return ...

P.S. I have been obliged to draw for the journey.

As his gondola glided past the Doge's Palace, and entered the Grand Canal on its way to the mainland, giving him a last view of the Piazetta, the Clock Tower and St Mark's, William had no regrets at leaving the confined atmosphere of the city. Venice in the eighteenth century was much as it had been centuries. On the debit side were the smells and the dirt: even the Doge's Palace was filled with 'stinking water', through which the nobles, 'who honestly contribute their share', paddled with uplifted gowns; the immorality: the city was known as the 'brothel of Europe' – courtesans, wearing bright colours to distinguish themselves from the other quietly-dressed citizens, stood by the dozen, 'with their breasts open and their faces all bedaubed with paint', at the doors and windows 'to invite their customers'. On the credit side was – besides the masterpieces of architecture and art – the wonderful virile activity that composed the scene on the Square of St Mark: here might be seen all sorts of fashions, might be heard all the languages under the sun; here in the evening came all the world to see and be seen – Jews, Turks, and Christians; lawyers, knaves, and pickpockets; mountebanks, old women, and physicians; women of quality, with masks; strumpets barefaced; in short, such a jumble of senators, citizens, gondoliers, and people of every character and condition, 'that your ideas are broken, bruised, and dislocated in the crowd, in such a manner, that you can think, or reflect, on nothing; yet this being a state of mind which many people are fond of, the place never fails to be well attended, and, in fine weather, numbers pass a great part of the night there'. When the piazza was illuminated, and the shops in the adjacent streets were lighted up, the whole had a brilliant effect; and as ladies as well as gentlemen frequented the casinos and coffee-houses, the life on the Square of St Mark may well have reminded William of that at Vauxhall or Ranelagh.

So William sailed away in his gondola; perhaps at noon, when the beautiful deep-sounding bells of St Mark's Campanile are rung, and the great gun is fired, and the startled pigeons rise in a cloud.

9

VIENNA

Mountains and river valleys lie on either side of the road from Venice to Vienna. William now entered a scene utterly different from any that he had met with in Italy. Diverse as the Italian landscape is – the flat Roman plains dotted with classical ruins, white slow-footed oxen and umbrella pines; the green hills and cypresses of Tuscany – nothing that William had so far seen was in any way related to the natural surroundings in which he now found himself. Here the mountains, covered from foot to peak with sweet-smelling fir trees, rose high about him on all sides. Drifting through the clear air hung smoke from autumnal bonfires. Little apple-green lakes lay among the high hills. The roads, fenced with untrimmed wood cut from the neighbouring trees, were good; but rickety wooden bridges spanning ravines could bring disaster if not carefully crossed.

The road through Friuli and the Austrian Duchy of Carniola led north of the great Karawanken mountains, passing by the peaceful waters of the Worthersee; beyond Klagenfurt it ran in a north-easterly direction along the valley of the river Mur to the Semmering Pass and descended through the Vienna woods into the imperial city.

> Vienna, the 14th of November, 1768. My dearest Mother, In my last of the 28th of October I mentioned my setting out for this city, where I arrived last night after a long and tedious journey, owing to the bad weather, which we had almost all the way, as it was either fog or rain; so I could have no pleasure in the looking out of the coach window. But when fair we passed thro' some most beautiful spots, the whole journey being almost in the mountains, which are covered with wood up to the top. We passed thro' many beautiful valleys and followed the course of a delightful river for near twenty English miles.

The influence of Vienna as the capital of the Empire cannot be overestimated. The Empire was by far the most important of the great European powers. Although weakened by the Seven Years' War, its dominions were vast, and potential strength enough to keep Catherine of Russia and Frederick of Prussia guessing. For centuries it had been the leader of the Germanic element in Europe. The present ruler, Maria Theresa, had been sickened by the suffering and waste of the Seven Years' War. Her son Joseph, Emperor and Co-Regent with his mother, although more liberal-minded than the Empress in religious and social affairs, has so far had no direct experience of war. Possessing an active and aggressive mind, and in control of the army, his thoughts were occupied with the aggrandisement of his country. The Co-Regency was, indeed, a delicately-balanced arrangement. Maria Theresa, strong, traditional and religious; Joseph, determined, progressive and liberal – this mother and her son lived and worked in a state of tension and conflict, and it was only their absolute devotion to each other that made the Co-Regency possible.

William continued his letter of 14 November:

> As yet I cannot give you any account of the town, but everything seems to be very magnificent, by the little that I have seen. It seems to be a second Paris in regard to dress, only rather more magnificent. As yet I have not been presented at Court nor in any of the houses. Tomorrow I am to be presented to some of the great people and the next day at Court. Lord Stromont* seems inclined to be very civil and to make this place agreeable. I make no doubt but that I shall spend my time very well. If I should be a little neglectful in writing for this next week or a fortnight it will be owing to visiting or one thing or another till I am settled. I, thank God, am mighty well, and so is Bolle ... I hope in my next to give you some account of this place.

Although William had spent only one night in the city, he had already observed what was one of Vienna's most striking characteristics – the influence of Paris on the noble Viennese families, who, with their great wealth, surpassed that city in splendour. The French language was spoken, French manners prevailed in the gay crowded salons, French fashions were followed. Dressed dolls were regularly sent from Paris for the purpose of teaching the women how to put on their dresses and arrange their hair. Even the men periodically got reports from Paris, which they laid before their hairdressers and tailors. The equipages and horses were most splendid. The nobility, enormously wealthy, lived in great luxury. The dinners they gave became feasts at which twenty different kinds of wine would be

* British Ambassador of Vienna.

served, a note being laid on each plate mentioning every sort that might be called for. Since the great families were well disposed towards Englishmen, William could look forward to being entertained hospitably, and to meeting intelligent men and accomplished women.

Driving through the streets on his way to visit some of these 'great people', William would have passed through a throng of coaches belonging to persons of wealth from all over the Empire. On these coaches sat servants wearing colourful national dress. Mounted on grey horses with silver bridles and green trappings the Hungarian Life Guard would ride by, magnificently dressed in scarlet Hussar uniforms laced with silver. Arrived at the homes of the nobility, William found that they lived in splendid palaces – some of the most splendid in Europe. Vienna had recently been adorned with many fine buildings and gardens. Two of the most famous architects responsible for these were Fischer von Erlach and Lukas von Hildebrandt. The Trinity Column in the Graben, the Karlskirche and the Hofburg Library are the outstanding achievements of Fischer von Erlach. Of Hildebrandt's works the most famous are the Upper and Lower Belvedere, connected by a garden of tall, clipped hedges, flights of steps and statues – built as the Summer Palace of Prince Eugene. The most successful of the other buildings in and around Vienna – built, as were the foregoing, in the baroque style – are the Summer Palace of Prince Liechtenstein, with its garden and its magnificent collection of pictures, and the Empress' Summer Palace of Schonbrunn. At Schonbrunn Maria Theresa and her family, surrounded by nobles attached to the Court, wandered on cool summer evenings in the shade of the high clipped hornbeam hedges and along the tree-lined alleys. The courtiers were dressed in the latest Paris fashions, the ladies in enormous hooped skirts of brocade and ribbons, their powdered hair surmounted by ostrich plumes, the gentlemen in coloured silk coats and knee breeches.

Two years previously (1766) Joseph II had thrown open the Prater to the inhabitants of Vienna. The great tree-filled park bordering the Danube had become the most popular pleasure-ground. Here on summer evenings the ladies and gentlemen appeared in carved gilt coaches and together with crowds of less wealthy people watched firework displays.

Of pre-baroque Vienna the dominating landmark was, then as now, the Gothic cathedral of St Stephen, with its steep roof, its single spire, and its deep C tone bell – the Pummerin, which, dedicated to peace, was cast in 1711 after the victorious end of the Austro-Turkish war. The old city walls stood where now lies the Ringstrasse; these walls marked the limits of the capital, and enclosed a mass of narrow, crooked streets.

A fortnight after his arrival William was able to give some account of his activities:

> 1st of December, 1768 ... Yesterday ... I was taken up all morning seeing the Knights of the Golden Fleece dine in public, and the Emperor at the head of them all dressed in their robes. The Emperor is a mighty well looking man, especially in his robes. As for the Empress Queen, I have not yet seen her, as she is very retired and lives mostly in a family way. I have seen two of her daughters, which are mighty handsome, especially the young one that is to be married to the Dauphin; but she is still very young. She seems to be the Emperor's favourite, as he generally takes her into his own box at the theatre, where he is always incognito, as he cannot bear any form or fuss. He dresses always in regimentals, and lives a great deal with his mother.

Marie Antoinette – 'the young one that is to be married to the Dauphin' – was at this time thirteen years old; two years later she married the future King Louis XVI of France.

The theatre at Vienna was famous throughout Europe. Indeed, in drama and music Vienna led the way. With Munich and Dresden it shared the distinction of presenting Italian opera most brilliantly.

> I have not seen the Prince Lobkowitz, as he lives almost always in the country, but they say he intends coming to town this winter. His sister is one of the most civil women, and has been very civil to me. It is a very agreeable house and has two amiable daughters, one of them beautiful and the other as agreeable as her sister is beautiful.

Lobkowitz was that same prince who had been a friend of William's mother when they were both young.

> I cannot say that this is the most agreeable place in the world, tho' it shines in good dinners and plenty, as I have dined but once or twice at home since I have been here.
>
> I wonder that none of the young ladies ever mentioning in their letters of a Count Zinzendorf having been at Carton. His brother has been to visit me and told me how sensible he was *de tous les politesse que*

Mon. le Duc avait montré a son frere a la campagne, etc., etc., and told me that his brother is delighted with Carton. He is one of the most agreeable men here. There is a Madame Degelfeld, the Dutch Minister's wife, that says she knew you in Holland; upon the strength of which she has been mighty civil to me. There are also some others which I mentioned in Emily's letter of the 23rd of November.

11th of December ... I continue mighty well, and am very well contented with me present situation, tho' the amusements are not the most lively, but they shine in good dinners. The ladies are mighty civil, agreeable and well bred; and what is extraordinary there are none of them very ugly nor very handsome. The handsomest lady here is a niece of Prince Lobkowitz. He is still in the country, but they say he'll be in town soon. His sister is a mighty good kind of a woman and has, as I above mentioned, a beautiful daughter and another who makes up for her sister's beauty by her sense and agreeableness. The men are most of them the dullest mortals that ever existed; I do not think I have met with five agreeable men of the country. One of the best of them is Count Zinzendorf, whose brother he told me was at Carton and admired the Hermitage, by which I suppose he means Waterstown.[*]

   Prince Kaunitz, who is the Prime Minister, is also very civil, especially to the English; which at present are not very numerous, as there is only one, who is an agreeable man and *beaucoup repandus dans le grand monde.* I thank my stars that I am not at Naples this Carnival, as there will be at least sixty English; there are, I may venture to say, near a hundred of them in Italy.

The Austrian Chancellor and diplomatist, Prince von Kaunitz was, from 1750 till his retirement in 1792, the dominating figure in the politics of eastern and central Europe.

There is here General Walmoden, a son of Lady Yarmouth's; he is Minister from Hanover; he is also an agreeable man, and his wife a mighty good woman. They have a little boy so like what Eddy[**] was when I left Ireland; he is bred up like an English child, and he is charming. Last time I saw him I played with him for an hour, to the great surprise of all the company.

General Johann Ludwig von Wollmoden was, reputedly, the son of

* A shell cottage in the grounds of Carton.
** William's brother, Lord Edward FitzGerald, for whom he had a great affection. Lord Edward grew up to become the famous Irish patriot.

George II. His mother, Amelie Sophie von Wallmoden, had been George's mistress, and had been created Countess of Yarmouth.

> I beg when you or any of the family write that you'll put on the direction 'by Ostende' as I get them much sooner, or otherways they come thro' France or Holland.

Christmas was now drawing near. William's life in Vienna went on much as usual, with a great many dinner parties. One of his ambitions – to be presented at Court – had not as yet been fulfilled.

> 21st of December, 1768 ... It being so near Xmas that I must wish you a merry one and a happy new year; it certainly will be a happy one for me, as I flatter myself I shall have the pleasure of seeing you and all the family. Tho' I amuse myself as well as possible abroad, yet the being so long absent, makes me very impatient to return ... The cold agrees mighty well with me, tho' as yet we have had no very cold weather. We have had some snow but it did not last; but I am in hopes that it will begin again, that we may have *traineaus*.
>
> I am very happy to find that the Duke of Leinster is contented with me. I flatter myself that I shall never give him reason to be otherways; I can assure you I study as much economy as is possible with decency. To be sure this place will run away with a good deal, tho' in the article of eating I hope will not ruin me; as yet I never dine at home and could have three or four dinners a day, as I am constantly asked to two places. To be sure, they live mighty well here, but one eats too much, as they bring you dish after dish as fast as you can eat. Tho', thank my stars, there is no suppers, or I don't know what would become of me, especially as I have entirely left off supping, which I think has been of service to me.
>
> I believe I shall never be presented at Court, as there has been no occasion since I have been here. The Empress lives a retired life, and the Emperor one only sees at the theatre, which at present is shut, which is a great loss here, for I never was yet in town where a theatre is so much wanted; but I hope we shall have it open again in a few days.

By the end of December William was able to formulate his plans for the spring:

> 31st of December, ('68) ... I propose leaving this if possible in the latter end of February or the beginning of March. From this I propose going to Dresden, where I shall stay at least a fortnight, as there is much

to see there. Amongst other things there is the finest collection of paintings in Europe. As to Berlin, I can't determine, as that depends upon the time I leave this, as it'll at least retard my projects three weeks or a month; and I look upon it to be necessary to be at Barèges in May, especially as I suppose you intend that I should be in Ireland in September. After Barèges I don't desire to stop anywhere excepting a week or so at Paris. I hope in your next you'll be so kind as to let me know that time you really expect me, in that I may determine accordingly ...

Tomorrow all the world is in their finery, as it is the only day of the year that the Court appear in their magnificence. I hope tomorrow to be presented to their Majesties and in my next will describe you the Court.

Your letter to Bolle gave me great pleasure. He shewed me that the Duke of Leinster and you were contented with us, especially in regard to money matters. I am afraid this quarter will be exorbitant, especially a tailor's bill, as I was obliged to make a fine suit for tomorrow, which I am afraid will come very high. But I flatter myself that the next quarter will be less, as I shall have paid off my tailor, and flatter myself that I shall want nothing but a frock between this and next winter. As yet we have had no cold, and very little snow. Letters from Italy mention its being extraordinary cold, and from Russia they write that the cold at present is not colder than what they have generally in October ... P.S. I am grieved to tell you upon a small calculation that Bolle and I have made this quarter amounts to a great deal more than I could expect. To be sure, my coat runs away with the greatest part.

New Year's Day, 1769, was celebrated with a splendid Court function, which William attended. He describes his presentation to Joseph II and Maria Theresa. But before he could find time to write, he was struck down with jaundice. And so an account of his illness occupies the first part of this letter:

January the 7th, 1769. I promised you in my last of the 31st of December to give you some account of the Court here, but I'll begin by giving you an account of myself first; which is that on the 5th instant, after a hearty breakfast and a good walk, I found myself to be yellow instead of my fine natural bloom. I immediately enquired for the best physician here, who told me that it was inclining to the yellow jaundice, and desires me to keep house; which I have accordingly done these two days past. I am in all other respects as well as ever, having no fever, nor any of the other symptoms of the jaundice than that everything I do is yellow. The physician flatters me that it'll be of no consequence provided that I take care of myself; so intend keeping the house until I get my natural colour ...

I was, according as I mentioned in my last, presented at Court on New Year's day, which is the greatest Court day here. To be sure, there was great magnificence. I was presented first to the Emperor, who did not say a word, as he is very bashful, and did not like being in his finery, tho' he had two diamond stars on and diamond fleece and buttons and his ribbon covered with diamonds.

The Empress was in mourning, as she is always in black since the death of the late Emperor. She has hardly any remains of beauty, and looks more like a fat housekeeper than an Empress; but she talked more than any of the rest. But she was hurried and wanted to get the ceremony of the day over, as she had been dressed ever since daylight, having her hand kissed by everybody. Her daughters are mighty handsome, especially the one married to Prince Albert of Saxony; the future Duchess of Parma is also a fine woman. La Dauphine was not there, as she was indisposed; nor the eldest, which is very ugly.

The Empress had lost her beauty eighteen months earlier when she had suffered severely from smallpox, only her eyes remained unaffected. The 'late Emperor' was, of course, Francis I, Maria Theresa's husband, who had died in 1765. The two daughters whom William mentions as having been present at Court were the Arch-duchesses Maria Christina, who was the wife of Albert, Duke of Saxe-Teschen, and Maria Amalia, who later married Ferdinand, Duke of Parma.

William continued to describe the Court:

There was many rich dresses and the ladies in general are well furnished with diamonds; as also the men, as most of them have the stars of their different orders in diamonds, which make a great figure, but I can't say look well upon men.

My coat was very handsome, and cost me a great deal of money, tho' upon such an occasion I could hardly have done without it. I flatter myself that it'll meet with your approbation when you see it; as that and another are the only coats, perhaps, worthy of carrying over. I suppose the Duke of Leinster would not have me bring home a wardrobe, nor would I choose the trouble of it; nor shall I have more than two winter suits. As for summer ones, they are little necessary in our country. I am very uneasy at the thoughts of this quarter, for it is enormous; but I flatter myself that the next will make amends.

It is a long while since I have heard from Ireland, but I see by the English papers that there are many mails due.

William continued to be visited by his doctor and a week later he had nearly recovered from his illness:

14th of January, 1769. I can with pleasure assure of my being much better than when I wrote last, tho' I can't say that I am perfectly re-established, as I have not entirely recovered my usual bloom. But I hope in a few days to get quite well, especially as I am tired of staying at home; but have been very lucky in escaping a fever, which I am told generally attends the jaundice. I have got a mighty good physician and have laid my whole state of health before him. He approves much of my drinking some waters this summer, but says he can't recommend Barèges, as he is not acquainted with the waters. He talks of Spa or Pyomont, but I made some kind of objection (tho' it would be more convenient), which was that if I went to Spa I should find so many acquaintances that I have not seen since I left England, that might cause an irregularity in the drinking of the waters, which he said was a very good reason. He told me that he would look over his papers, as he thinks he has one that treats upon the Barèges waters. But he has not yet given us an answer. Bolle is for Barèges, as he thinks that the heat may help to clear the blood. But I shall desire him to write you his opinion next post, as our time begins to draw near. I have thoughts of leaving this some weeks sooner than I first intended, as when at Dresden I shall be greatly tempted to see Berlin; and by setting out a fortnight or three weeks sooner, I flatter myself shall be able to do it with ease, and be at Barèges at the time I proposed at first. I hope my father will have no objection, and the King of Prussia is worth seeing as well as the town of Berlin.

There are at present a number of Irish officers in town; so you may be sure I am not much alone. We have here a Count Mahony, a broth-er-in-law of the Countess that is at Naples, who is Ambassador from Spain, who is one of the most agreeable, civil, obliging men I ever met with; he is adored by everybody that knows him. He comes here very often, and is most excellent company, as his conversation is sensible and agreeable.

The Carnival is begun, but I do not hear of its being very lively. This Court, which formerly was so lively, is now the dullest. The Emperor, tho' a young man, does not seem to care for any amusement.

Four days later William was giving his mother the good news that he had shaken off the jaundice:

18th of January, 1769. I can with pleasure assure you of my being quite

recovered of my late indisposition, and have been out airing this day for
the first time, and I hope to begin to go about tomorrow or next day;
which I can assure you I shall not be sorry for, as I am quite tired of
staying at home, tho' I must say the people have kindness enough not
to leave me much alone.

In spite of the many activities, social and otherwise, that occupied
him on his travels, William had not forgotten Miss Caroline
FitzGerald in faraway Ireland. He was glad to receive now a letter
from Lady Holland, 'which gives me hopes that you have some particular reason for not believing the general talk of Lord Kingsbro's
marriage, as I hear it is much talked of in Ireland'. On his father being
created, some months previously, Earl of Kingston, Robert King was
styled Viscount Kingsborough. But William was not so sanguine:
'There surely must be something in it, as I have even heard of it from
some of the Irish officers here; so I doubt by a thing being so univer-
sal must have some foundation'. William goes on to express his desire
for marriage with the young woman, especially as his mother seemed
also to wish it. 'Worst come to the worst,' he concluded, 'the being
refused would be better than never having proposed'.

On the last night of the Carnival William caught a slight cold,
which, however, did not confine him to his house. He was anxious to
continue his journey, as Vienna had now become very dull. He wanted to get on to Dresden, and so to Berlin. By setting out early from
Vienna, he hoped to stay a fortnight or three weeks in each of these
places. He asked that his letters be directed *chez le Comte Joseph
Bobza, Banquier, a Dresde.*

I am told [wrote William on 11 February] that Madame de Barré,* who
has succeeded Madame Pompadour in the King of France's affections,
is a relation of Lord Barrymore's, at least he has owned her as one. I hear
she is made Duchess of Luce. We have at present here two or three
Polish ladies on their return to Poland; they are reckoned beauties, but
I cannot say much for them.

About this time Bolle became unwell, which delayed William's
departure.

22nd February, 1769. I write these few lines to acquaint you of my

* du Barry.

being in perfect health and propose leaving this as soon as Bolle is perfectly established, which I hope will be in a few days. I cannot say I shall regret Vienna much, as it is not the most agreeable place I have been in since I left you. We seem determined on the Barèges scheme, but propose going to Berlin for a few days only, and shall make no long stay anywhere till we get to Barèges. But being so near Berlin when at Dresden, that it would be a shame not to see it. What pleasure it is to me to think how near the time of seeing you approaches, which, to be sure, will be a great comfort ...

We have delightful weather, which I cannot say I am very glad of, as I am afraid it'll cause our having bad on our journey. This has been the mildest winter that ever was, to my sorrow, as I wanted to feel what great cold was, and to compare it to heat; secondly, for to have seen a *course de traineau*, which by all accounts is a very fine sight.

This town affords no very great things to attract the traveller's merit. At Dresden there is one of the finest collections of paintings in Europe, besides the china manufacture, etc. etc., and by all accounts a very pretty town, and this a very ugly one. By the time I can get an answer to this I shall be most likely on my departure from Berlin so you would oblige me by directing your next to me *chez Mess. Jacob Gontard & fils a Francfort sur le Mayn*, which will be the surest place for me, as it may wait there till I come.

February drew to a close, and William was nearly ready to leave Vienna.

1st of March, 1769 ... We have the most delightful weather that ever was, which makes me long to get on the road, which I hope to do about this day sennight. Bolle is, thank God, much better, and I hope will be able to set out then.

I am very happy to find that my last year's money was not so extravagant as the former. I dread the last quarter as it was enormous. I hope we shall reduce this one, tho' the next will be to be apprehended, as we shall be so much on the road and we shall make no longer stay anywhere than a fortnight till we get to Barèges, which seems to be our scheme.

I can assure you that the good dinners have not fattened me at all, as I am quite a slender young man to what I was. I am very well, thank God, and long much to see you at Carton, which I hope will be in September. I flatter myself that I shall be at Barèges the beginning of June, where we must stay at least two months. I would not desire to make any stay at Paris unless it was for a whole winter, as then one might get some acquaintances amongst the French.

I suppose the Duke of Leinster does not wish me to bring home many clothes, for which I am at present wearing out those that I made in Italy, and shall have but one rich coat, which is one that I made here, which I flatter myself, when you see it, you'll say it is very handsome *et digne de mon fils.*

You make me very happy in regard to Miss*; it gives me still hopes that I may have a chance yet.

William's youngest aunt, Lady Cecilia Lennox, who died later this same year, aged twenty, was ill with consumption; William recommended that she be sent to the south of France:

I approve much of your sending Ciss abroad, as her disorder ought always to be taken in the beginning. I doubt not but Nice will be the place destined. I hope it may, as I am convinced that it is the best climate in Europe.

One sees very little of the Empress, but her daughters, as I have mentioned before, are very handsome.

You'll be surprised at my changing my direction so often, but you'll be so kind as to direct to me *chez Mon. Frank Frères, Banquier, à Strasburg,* till you hear farther from me.

Once more Bolle removed William's fine clothes from the wardrobe, folded them up, and packed them neatly into the trunks. No doubt the suit he put away with the greatest care was the magnificent one William had bought for the Imperial Court on New Year's day. This was his newest coat, and he intended to show it to his mother for her approval when he got home. The other suits he was wearing out, and would not take home, with the exception perhaps of the one he had made for the Emperor's projected visit to Florence, or the handsome velvet coat he had bought for the King of Naples' birthday.

And so, with the great C note of St Stephen's bell ringing in his ears, and the laughter of the people in the Prater, and the clip-clopping of the horses that drew the stately gilded carriages, and the music of Haydn; with the memories of the Emperor in uniform sitting in his box at the theatre with his sister Marie Antoinette, and his mother Maria Theresa holding her Court and looking like a fat housekeeper; of the other handsome arch-duchesses, the luxurious dinners, his Imperial Majesty's gossiping Irish officers, the gardens of the

* Caroline FitzGerald.

Belvedere, fine weather – little snow and consequently no *traineaus* – and the Knights of the Golden Fleece dining in their robes; with these and other memories William and Bolle trundled in their carriage through the narrow Vienna streets, passed through the city gate, and followed the valley of the Danube northward.

10

PRAGUE – DRESDEN – BERLIN – BERNE
– LYONS

It was not usual for travellers in the eighteenth century to visit the German states, these being off the beaten track of the conventional Grand Tour. William's letters from these parts are, therefore, especially interesting.

The road from Vienna to Prague lay through Bohemia, and from Prague he wrote to his mother:

> Prague, the 13th of March, 1769. My dearest Mother, I must now return you many thanks for your long and obliging letter of the 7th of February, which I received a day or two before my departure from Vienna, which place I left the 10th instant and arrived here this very day, in perfect health, tho' I cannot say so much for Bolle, who is but indifferent, as he would travel all night on our first setting out, which he was too weak to bear; especially as we had very bad weather and the roads very bad owing to the snow that we had on the mountains and the rain in the bottoms.
>
> On our leaving Vienna we passed several branches of the Danube, which resemble more a lake than a river. But we soon got in the mountains, which we found covered with snow, so could not discover their beauty, otherways than their being a great deal of wood on the tops of them. Bohemia seems to be a fertile country and the ground lies well, its not being an entire plain; but it is greatly deficient in wood. I mean an open country where are no scattered trees, but here and there a forest, tho' not very large ones.

Of Prague William writes:

> Prague seems to be a fine town. It is situated in a valley with a large river running through it, which adds greatly, in my opinion, to the beauty of a town. It is much larger and handsomer than Vienna. By the accounts, and what I have seen of it as yet, I should not dislike spending some time here, if I had any time to spare. But as it is, I shall stay but a couple of

days; in which time I hope Bolle will be able to go on at easy days' journeys to Dresden. But he is so childish as to force himself. But if I see he
is not well enough, I shall remain a few days longer; but I flatter myself
he'll be well enough.

Prague was, indeed, a handsome city. The river Moldau was spanned
by a many-arched medieval bridge; there were strong city walls and
towers; there was a large number of baroque buildings; and on the
heights overlooking the city and the river was the historic palace of
the kings – the Hradschin. The people of Prague were famous for
their riches, the nobles living in greater luxury than in any other part
of central Europe. Every evening there was an assembly in one or
other of the palaces, where the guests amused themselves with gambling, and finished the night by sitting down to a feast of chicken,
pheasants, ortolans, trout, salmon and cray-fish, and good wine. Even
the least of the inns would provide the traveller with a meal of par-
tridge soup followed by a pheasant.

William had not much time to spend in Prague. Indeed, in spite
of the city's many attractions, he was anxious to push on; for he had
a long way to go before he reached his journey's end.

I am glad to find you approve of my Dresden and Berlin scheme, by
which means I shall have seen a great part of Germany and the King of
Prussia. To be sure, I shall be rather pressed for time, as we have a monstrous journey to take before we get to Barèges, where I should wish to
be as early in June as possible, that I may have full time to drink the
waters. In this journey through France there are but twenty miles that
I have seen before, which is from the Pont de St Esprit to Nîmes; which
is just the part of France I should wish to see again, as if you remember,
I was quite in love with the antiquities of Nîmes, which, to be sure, are
worth seeing twice. So you may imagine the great space of country I
have for to see before I shall see you, which I flatter myself will not be
long before. I can assure you I often think with pleasure how happy we
shall be at Carton, I hope some time before the Parliament meets; as
when in Dublin somehow or other one does not see one another so
comfortably as in country ...

Bolle begs his respects. I hope he'll be well rested in these two days;
halt, as I would willingly set off the 16th, as the 17th is St Patrick's day,
and this town swarms with Irish, and there is an Irish convent of
Franciscan friars who have a feast that day.

A few days later William took his leave of the baroque city, with its many cupolas glinting in the sun and its grand river Moldau. Driving northward along the valley of the river Elbe, with the Erz Gebirge to the West, he entered Saxony and made for the capital.

William's first impressions of Dresden were of tall stone houses and broad, straight, well-paved streets crowded with Germans and Poles. The most interesting building was the Zwinger, built between 1711 and 1722 by Poeppelmann, the architect of Augustus II, King of Poland and Elector of Saxony. The Zwinger was all that was built of a project for a great palace and garden that would have stretched 200 or 300 yards down to the banks of the Elbe. The Zwinger was the courtyard of this proposed palace, and consisted of a great court surrounded by a gallery and seven pavilions, embellished with fantastic sculpture. This courtyard was usually filled with an animated crowd of colourfully dressed people; while up and down moved the magnificent coaches and fine horses of the rich. For in spite of the devastation caused by the Seven Years' War, and the financial losses which it brought about, the Saxons were still, by comparison with other central Europeans, a wealthy people. Their country was one of the richest states in Germany; and the Electors had built up a remarkably fine collection of pictures and gems. The picture gallery was, indeed, one of the greatest in Europe, and contained more than 2,000 paintings. Among these were Raphael's Sistine Madonna, and Coreggio's 'La Notte' and 'Mary Magdalene'.

> Dresden, the 25th of March, 1769 ... I cannot give you any account of the society at Dresden, as the people have been in devotion this week past, and the Court have the measles. So I have no authority to describe to you any of the royal family, as I have only seen them *en passans*.
>
> As for the picture gallery, it is the most curious I ever met with. There are in one of the rooms upwards of two hundred original pictures of the first Italian Masters, and out of that number one can hardly say there is one indifferent one. I have not yet seen any china or its manufacture, but propose seeing it this next week, and hope in my next to give you a better account of Dresden and its environs, and especially of the china manufacture, which is at twelve English miles distance.
>
> It is terrible here to see the destruction of the King of Prussia. He has ruined certainly the most beautiful town that ever was, and has by the strength of his canon laid half the town in ruin, tho' they are building it up very quick. The Elbe runs very prettily thro' the town, and there is a beautiful bridge over it.
>
> I propose staying here ten days or a week longer, and then proceed to Berlin ... Excuse the blunders and the ill writing of this letter as I am

half asleep and the post goes out tomorrow morning early.

The country around Dresden was very charming, and William made a point of seeing it. The main object of his excursion was the china factory at Meissen. It is interesting to note that as late as the seventh decade of the eighteenth century the old tradition of secrecy regarding pottery and notably kiln design was still strong, since William tells us that he was kept away from the preparatory processes – i.e. the mixing of the material and what he calls 'the baking'.*

> Dresden, the 1st of April, 1769 ... I am just now returned from an agreeable jaunt to Meissen, a town about twelve miles from this, where the china manufacture is carried on. I must say the journey is worth taking were it nothing else to see but the country, which must be more beautiful in summer time when the verdure appears. The road follows the course of the river Elbe, which is very delightful.
>
> The town is not worth mentioning. The manufacture is carried on in an old castle belonging to the Elector of Saxony, where there are upwards of seven hundred workmen and women employed. We went thro' most of the different branches. The preparing of the clay, the polishing and the baking they let nobody see. But I saw the painters and the moulding part of it, which is curious. Think of the china cups and saucers etc, etc., which you see, must go thro; four or five different hands before it is finished. I was much surprised at finding many girls painting. I afterward was in the warehouses, where, to be sure, I saw some most beautiful china; and must say had I been rich I should have had a great pleasure in regaling you with a specimen of their manufacture. To be sure, it is immensely dear, or otherways I should have been tempted, and had no other reason for not doing it than that of keeping down this next quarter, which will in all probability rise on account of my travelling a good deal. But I hope my father will be content with this quarter, and flatter myself that I shall be able to reduce this year.

The reigning Elector of Saxony, whom William mentions as owning the old castle in which the china manufacture was carried on, was Frederick Augustus (1750-1827), son of the Elector Frederick Christian. He had succeeded in 1763. He became, as Frederick Augustus I, the first King of Saxony in 1806.

* See Frank Davis' article, 'Birds in Porcelain', *Illustrated London News,* 19 August 1950.

I propose leaving this the 6th of this month for Berlin. I should willingly have remained here some time longer, as it is a beautiful town, and many things worthy of a traveller's notice. Amongst what I have already mentioned in my former letters, there is the finest collection of prints in Europe, and the most rare; there are surely some hundreds of volumes. I must not forget to mention the Palais d'Hollande, which is one of the Elector's Palaces which was built by Augustus the 2nd, King of Poland, and intended to be furnished entirely with china ...* there, to be sure the greatest quantity ...* I ever saw, and amongst it some of ...* beautiful blue and white vases of what you call old china and very large. I could have put one in my pocket for you were it not they were fitter to hold me than me to carry them. There is also a great deal of very fine Japan.

All this was near going to ruin in the time of the siege as there is the marks of some cannon balls still in the walls. It is dreadful to see the havoc his Prussian Majesty has made in this beautiful town.

There is still more eating in this town than Vienna, as they are in the way of giving great suppers as well as dinners ...

Pray, tell the Duke of Leinster that it is reported here this day that our Ambassador at Constantinople has been sent to the Seven Towers, where the Russian one is already confined. This news is not absolutely affirmed.

John Murray had been appointed British Ambassador to Turkey in 1766, arriving at Constantinople that same year. He sailed from Constantinople on leave in May 1775, and died at Venice the following August. There is a great mass of his correspondence with British Agents at Vienna in the State Papers.

With much reluctance William left Dresden. In his own opinion, he had been able to spend but far too short a time there. The city was, indeed, one of the most agreeable in Germany. It was William's misfortune that he had been unable to enjoy the pleasures of the Court on account of the measles. The Court was for a time counted one of the most brilliant in Europe. And the Court band, the theatre, and the dancers were maintained at enormous expense. Leaving the fair Saxon capital, with its tall stone houses and streets full of gaily dressed Poles and Germans, William's carriage pulled out into the countryside, along the wretched roads of Germany.

The German roads were some of the worst in Europe. Post wagons did not make over eighteen miles a day. Many of the roads

* Manuscript torn.

consisted of loose sand, into which the wheels sank up to the axle-tree. William found the journey from Dresden to Berlin uncomfortable enough:

> Berlin, the 15th of April, 1769. I can with pleasure assure you of my being arrived here in perfect health after a short but disagreeable journey thro' a very ugly sandy country. So a course it was very tedious, as one could not go out of a foot's pace, and, to render it more agreeable, we were delayed twelve hours at a bad inn on account of the passing of the Elector of Saxony.

Germany, being composed of petty states, had never had a capital. But Berlin, though small compared with Vienna, Paris or London, was even at this time one of the first cities of Europe. The streets were broad and spacious; the houses neat, low, and built of a fine white freestone. There was the royal palace, churches, the arsenal, the opera house. (Unlike many other German cities, there were no old buildings.) Already the most fashionable walk was along the Unter den Linden. Surrounding the city was a wall and fortifications.

French influence was strong – the French language was as commonly spoken and understood as German – for two reasons: Firstly, the encouragement given by Frederick the Great to everything French; and secondly, partly as a result of the King's attitude, the great influx to the capital of French refugees. Many people in fact called Berlin the Paris of Germany.

Although there was as yet no university in Berlin, the city was a centre of great intellectual activity. Lessing had recently published his two masterpieces, *Laokoon* and *Minna von Barnhelm*. Having spent several years in Berlin at different times, he had helped to make the city widely recognised for is enlightenment. Drawing his inspiration from English literature rather than from the French, he was doing much to emancipate the German drama and to give Germany for a time, the first place in the intellectual life of the world. He had asserted the superiority of Shakespeare to Corneille, Racine and Voltaire, and his criticism of Voltaire had led Frederick to exclude him from all public appointment. Frederick was, indeed, passionately devoted to French literature. He in no way encouraged his own countrymen, and was incapable of appreciating the rising German writers that were to make his reign illustrious. In the realm of politics, however, the King was giving to Prussia that supremacy which inevitably brought with it an advance in all forms of culture.

A little to the west of Berlin was the Schloss at Charlottenburg, with its lovely rococo decorations. And beyond again, Potsdam. It was here that Frederick gathered about him some of the most brilliant minds of Europe. The three palaces at Potsdam were the Town Palace, the New Palace, and Sanssouci, all built by Frederick. The New Palace he erected out of ostentation during the Seven Years' War. The interior contained beautiful boiseried rooms decorated in silver and gold, contemporary French furniture, and pictures by Watteau. The French art of the period was to be found here in its most perfect form. Sanssouci, much smaller, was a creation of equal perfection.

> I have not seen enough of Berlin to give you a thorough description of it. All I have to say about it is that it is a very large town regularly built and very large streets, but very empty, as one sees nothing but soldiers, which are swarming about like a pack of bees about a beehive.
>
> The King is at Potsdam, where seldom a foreigner is presented to him. But I intend seeing him as he goes to the parade. The rest of the family I shall be presented to tomorrow, so I hope in my next I shall be able to give you an account of them.[*]
>
> I do not propose making any longer stay here than at Dresden, for it does not seem so agreeable a place; nor is the country about it so fine, nor is there so many things worthy of notice.
>
> I have met with Baron Kniphausen, who you must have known in England, as he used to make Lady Barrymore's party at loo.

Baron von Kniphausen had been Prussian Ambassador in London. Margaret, Countess of Barrymore, was an old friend of the Duchess of Leinster, and a great card player. She outlived both her son and daughter-in-law, dying in 1788.

> I received a present from the Elector of Saxony of a gold medal that was struck on the occasion of his receiving the homages, at Dresden.
>
> I have not heard from you for some time, but expect to find letters from you at Frankfurt, which is the next place I am bound to; and shall stop nowhere but a day or two at Hanau to see our Princess Mary, the Landgrave of Hesse Cassel's wife, and sister to the Princess Emily. I am told she takes it very kind of any Englishman that stops to see her.

---

[*] Not extant.

'Our' Princess Mary was the fourth daughter of George II. Born in 1723, she had married in 1740 Frederick William, Hereditary Prince of Hesse, who succeeded at Landgrave of Hesse-Cassel in 1760. She separated from him on his turning Roman Catholic in 1754, and resided with her children at Hanau. She lived until 1772. The princes of the house of Hesse-Cassel possessed great wealth, which was partly derived from their system of hiring out their subjects as soldiers to foreign powers.

> I am told there is nothing to stop me at Frankfurt, so I shall go on immediately to Mannheim, which they tell me is the most agreeable Court in Germany.
>
> Berlin, the 22nd of April, 1769 ... I propose leaving this tomorrow morning for Frankfurt, where I flatter myself that I shall find letters of a fresher date. I propose taking Potsdam in my way, where I hope to get a peep at the King, but cannot be presented to him as he sees no strangers there. I have seen the rest of the royal family and will send you an account of them in my next, as I have not time at present. Nor should I have wrote, were it not to let you know that I am very well, and that I think Bolle is better than he has been, but not so well as I could wish.

Passing through Frankfurt William saw a great bustle of activity: prosperous citizens thronging the streets; Jews wearing distinctive pieces of yellow cloth. The old city was at the junction of many main roads which led to all parts of Germany. Here was held the great annual fair. Here too was the book selling and publishing centre. For many centuries the coronation of the Holy Roman Emperors had taken place in the city.

Along with other cities of the upper Rhine, Mannheim had been bombarded and destroyed by the French in 1689. It was rebuilt ten years later with geometrical regularity: straight streets crossed one another at right angles. The Electors Palatine had left their original capital, Heidelberg, in 1720, and moved to Mannheim, where they built an enormous palace of little architectural interest. This palace contained one of the most famous collections of art and antiquities in Germany, its chief rivals being those at Dusseldorf and at Dresden. If William spent long enough in Mannheim to go to the Court, he may also have had time to look at something more worth seeing architecturally than the palace: the Church of St Ignatius, a good example of its kind, and due to Alessandro Galli Bibbiena, who died an old man this same year (1769).

The scene that lay before William as he travelled along the banks of the Rhine was one of hills covered with vineyards, and of ancient walled towns. All the towns were interesting and picturesque; many, however, had suffered severely in war. And as William's carriage rattled through the narrow streets he found these streets dirty and badly paved; and through the carriage window he saw that the old houses were almost tumbling down for want of repair.

Strasbourg was a French possession. Here William called for his letters; and no doubt had a look at the great cathedral. From Strasbourg he continued his journey up the Rhine, and entered Switzerland at Basle.

> Berne, the 14th of May, 1769. My dearest Mother, You may see by my date that I am thus far advanced in my way to Barèges, being exceedingly pleased with my journey from Strasbourg here. Basle was the first town we entered in Switzerland. It is situated on the Rhine, which is of a great breadth. The town is large but ugly, otherways but its situation. From thence we passed to Soleure,* thro' a most beautiful country, but our weather was so bad that one could not enjoy the beautiful views.
>
> Yesterday we arrived here (our weather being better), so profited more of the delightful country. The valleys were high perfection, as the rain had given them the spring verdure; the mountains covered with wood, the plains and rising grounds either cultivated or pasture land, with many trees scattered about; amongst them many cherry trees which were in blossom, which rendered the objects still more enchanting.
>
> Berne is situated on a ridge of hills with a beautiful river running close under, tho' in the most delightful serpentine. The walks about the town are charming. In one of them you see two different views of the river which one can hardly believe to be the same. The hills about it are covered with wood; what is not, is cultivated. [There are] many odd houses and villages in the environs, with a fine view of the Alps, which are still covered with snow, as we have had dreadful cold dry weather for some time past, as since I left Dresden till I arrived at Basle we had constant dry weather.

It is not surprising that William liked Berne. It had a pleasant social life, and the inhabitants were friendly towards foreigners. Here

* Ger. – Solothurn.

everything was simple. The sophistication of the fashionable assemblies of France and Italy was lacking; gambling was forbidden by law. Parties began about four or five o'clock in the afternoon and went on until eight, when the guests usually went home. Swiss cities in general were noted for an absence of luxury; remarkable considering the wealth and prosperity of the inhabitants. In Basle, for example, no citizen was allowed to have a servant behind his carriage; while in Zurich the use of a carriage was prohibited to everybody except strangers. In many parts of the country regulations concerning dress and deportment were in force. Lady Holland, who was in Switzerland at Geneva, almost exactly two years before William, made the following observations: 'Tis all bourgeois in this place, one sees everywhere industry, comfort and excessive cleanliness, very different from *la bella Italia* ... There are no beggars here, no stealing, no murders or disorders happen; everyone is employed, everyone obliged to keep in their own station, a particular dress for the maidservant which is neat and tidy, and which they must not transgress on any account.'

> I propose going from this to Lausanne. I wanted Bolle to go to Neuchatel, but he does not care to go, as he says it would cost him too much money, as he has many poor relations who would expect him to be very rich, as he is with a *My Lord anglais*, who all foreigners think is made of money and that his people are also. It is terrible how one is obliged to squabble and bargain for everything. He is better than he was, though not so well as I could wish.
>
> I do [not] know where to desire you to direct to me, as I do not know any address, but I will let you know from Geneva. I hope to be at Barèges the second week in June. As yet, thank God, am mighty well. ... How I long for September! Pray, do you intend that I should make any stay in England at my return, or whether I shall go immediately to Ireland? I hope the latter. My travelling so much runs away with money; I was obliged to draw fifty pound at Strasbourg.

William wanted new clothes for the time when he would arrive home in Ireland, so he asked his mother to get his sister, Emily, to make the necessary arrangements:

> I beg you will tell Emily that she must be so kind as to have fourteen plain shirts with good wristbands for to put lace ruffles to, and six plain ruffles shirts. I beg pardon for troubling you, but forgot to mention it in my last letter to her of the 7th of this month.

William, like his Aunt Lady Holland, possessed that rare thing among eighteenth-century travellers – an appreciation of mountain scenery. His journey through Switzerland was to him an uninterrupted delight. His coach, battered by the German roads but still holding together, swung along the road in the shadow of the Bernese Alps, along the shores of the Lake of Geneva by way of Lausanne. Looking out through the carriage window, over the backs of his sweating horses and impudent postillions, he saw the neat spring countryside, the cherry blossoms in flower, and the blue waters of the lake that stretched away to the mountains of Haute Savoie beyond.

William took the same road as did Lady Holland two years previously; and, as has already been said, he made the journey during the same month – May. It seems fitting, therefore, to include a descriptive passage from Lady Holland's own Letters: 'We went the first day's journey thro' the Pays de Vaud all by the Lake of Geneva. The day was fine, the roads good, the inns excellent, so that it was altogether delightful. Nothing can be more lovely than that Lake. The Pays de Vaud is in the canton of Bern, and as far as enjoying liberty and all the comforts of life can contribute to make people happy in this life, those people possess it. They have no taxes, no standing army, no monks, no priests, to molest them; great industry among them, affluence without luxury, and religion without superstition. To be sure, the Swiss may be reckoned the happiest people on this spot of ours. Their laws and regulations prevent luxury, which is generally the ruin of people at ease; before these troubles at Geneva, in which the French interfere, they were also very happy. I am glad I have seen them, I own; and I think after all were I obliged to live out of my own country I would fix somewhere among the Swiss; tho' perhaps in some respects Paris would amuse me more, yet I think a country house in the environs of Geneva or in the Pays de Vaud would be a more rational thing. My travels, sweet siss, make me see the misery caused by a superstitious religion and a great standing army in a light I never before saw it; to be sure priests and soldiers are the bane of human kind' and 'The environs of Geneva are full of country houses, vineyards, fields, and all looks so cheerful and so cultivated it gives one spirits to see them. The prospects of the mountains and the lake are beautiful. Except the prospects, which are great as well as cheerful, *tout est en petit* – houses, gardens, way of life ... The people in this country were too happy, and have quarelled among themselves, the people and the magistrates. The French have meddled in their quarrels as mediators, and they much fear their little republic will be ruined by it; such is the fate of all in this *bas monde*, neither liberty or plenty can secure happiness, and I much doubt whether poor Neapolitan lounging himself in the sun, who lives on chestnuts, don't enjoy as much happiness as the rich bourgeois of London or Geneva.

Geneva had the biggest population of any town in Switzerland – 24,000 inhabitants. The people were lively and courteous, their conversation was gay. In the summer they would have country parties outside the city walls; at dusk the sound of the drum from the ramparts would recall them to the town; for then the gates would be shut and could not be opened by the officer of the guard without an order from the Syndics, an order which could only be got in cases of great emergency.

From Geneva William took the road to Lyons – the city that had been virtually the starting-point of his Grand Tour three years earlier.

> Lyons, the 30th of May, 1769. My dearest Mother, You may see by the date that I am thus far advanced in my way to Barèges, where I hope to be in less than fourteen nights. I have been here between five and six days and propose remaining a day or two longer, as I have been obliged to change my carriage, as the German roads have been a great detriment to it. I have exchanged it for a two wheel chaise, by which I mean I save a horse and a postillion, and shall go much quicker.
>
> From Geneva here, some part of the road is beautiful as one passes two small lakes[*] and have several different views of the Rhône.
>
> I have already given you an account of Lyons. There are present several English, among which there is Lady Stanley, wife to Sir John.

Sir John Stanley, who was father of the first Lord Stanley of Alderley, married Margaret, daughter and heiress of Hugh Owen of Penrhos in Anglesey.

> There is also Mr and Mrs Kerr, who have two of Mrs George Pitt's daughters, which are really two fine girls; the eldest of them is like her mother and the other very like the father.

* Probably the Lac d'Annecy and the Lac du Bourget.

George Pitt, it has already been said, had been British Envoy to Turin. He and his beautiful wife, Penelope, had one son and three daughters. The eldest daughter Penelope, was already married to Colonel Edward Ligonier, who subsequently became Earl Ligonier; her marriage with Ligonier was, however, dissolved in 1772, and she later married a trooper in the Blues. The second daughter, Louisa, married Peter Beckford, and was mother of the third Baron Rivers. The third daughter, Marcia Lucy, married James Fox-Lane.

> From this I go to Toulouse, where you'll be so kind as to direct your letters during my stay at Barèges. I do [not] propose stopping there more than a day anywhere till I get there. I pass thro' Nîmes, so shall have the pleasure of seeing the antiquities there again. From thence to Montpelier. We have had no very hot weather as yet, and can assure you of my being very well.
>
> I forget whether I mentioned from Geneva my having been obliged to draw for money. I am afraid our running so much about will make this quarter run very high. I can assure you it gives me great uneasiness.
>
> Pray, my love to the Duke of Leinster and the rest of the family. Adieu, my dearest Mother, believe me ever your most affectionate son, KILDARE. Direct to me chez Mess. ?assiny Davaisse & Comp: à Toulouse.

There we must take our leave of William as letter-writer. For that is the last surviving of his Grand Tour letters. William probably left Barèges during the month of August, in order to be back in Ireland in time for the meeting of the new Parliament in October.

On his way home he passed through the Hague. The flat Dutch countryside, intersected with canals, and dotted with windmills, provided a strong contrast to some of the other countries William had recently seen – the cypress-covered hills of Tuscany, for example, or the mountains of Switzerland.

While at the Hague William went to see his great-aunt, Lady Margaret Bentinck and her husband. Lady Margaret was the younger daughter and co-heiress of William, Earl Cadogan, and wife of Charles John Bentinck, Count Bentinck. It is from the pen of Charles Bentinck that we catch our final glimpse of William, Lord Kildare, as a young man of twenty years completing the Grand Tour.

PRAGUE – DRESDEN – BERLIN – BERNE – LYONS

C. Bentinck to Duchess of Leinster:
Hague, December 12th, 1769. My dear Lady Duchess ... Since we had
the pleasure of seeing Lord Kildare here, I have put off from time to
time writing to your Grace on this subject, as I really was desirous to
do; I feared you would take my expressions with regard to him, too
much as a flattering compliment to you. At last I venture; but to avoid
all suspicion, I must first remind you that flattery never was my vice;
and that plain truth has made my way through the world much rougher
than it need have been, if I had been able to spare it.

Lord Kildare's visit here was as kind as it was unexpected. It seldom
happens nowadays that a young man coming from his travels has much
else to recommend him besides French clothes, a high touppee, per-
fumes, snuff boxes, toys and trinkets, awkward French airs, nonsense
and so forth. After having seen so much of this, I could not but admire
at first sight the plain and decent appearance and easy politeness of Lord
Kildare, and much more still his sense and knowledge when we came
to talk of the places and persons he had seen. I can truly venture to say
that I never saw a man of his age, nor several years older, that had travelled with as much judgment and attention, nor that seemed so much
improved by seeing the world, which to me is a proof of his good nature
as well as good sense.

In short, I protest it was the greatest pleasure I have had this great
while, to see him; and I was extremely sorry that he was obliged to leave
us so soon. My judgment is not particular; for Sir Jos. Yorke, who is not
easily pleased with everyone, was as much taken with Lord Kildare as I
was; and as constantly given the highest commendations of him.
Everybody here was equally pleased with him. I cannot but most hearti-
ly wish the Duke of Leinster and your Grace may both long enjoy the
satisfaction and blessing of such a son.

11

CONCLUSION

William's father, alas! did not live long to enjoy the 'satisfaction and blessing of such a son'. The Duke died in November, 1773, when William succeeded to the title as second Duke of Leinster. His mother, Emily, Duchess, however, outlived her son by many years, dying in 1814.

William was present at the opening of the new Parliament in October, 1769. The following year, on 2 March, 1770, he came of age. And in November, 1771, when he was 22 years old, his father gave him his independence with an allowance of £2,000 a year. 'Lord Kildare', wrote the Duke in a memorandum on the subject, 'in town, is to find himself, servant, horses, etc., etc, with lodgings, stabling, and everything for himself and them, and go when and where he pleases, to any part of the world'.

From the citizens of Dublin, whom he now represented in Parliament, he had already received many honours. Between 1767 and 1770 he had been presented with the freedom of several Guilds: silver boxes from the Saddlers and Cooks, a silver trowel from the Bricklayers, a gold thimble from the Tailors, a silver box from the Weavers, a silver box in the form of a book from the Guild of St Luke. In 1771 he was one of the mourners at the funeral of Dr Charles Lucas, the celebrated radical, the 'tribune of the people'. Thousands of Dubliners lined the streets through which the funeral procession passed. Already William was showing which way his political sympathies lay.

On the death of his father, William found himself, at the age of 24, with a widowed mother, eleven brothers and sisters, and an aged grandmother. His mother had been left Carton for life unless she married again, and an allowance of £400 a year for each of her children. The following year, 1774, William's mother, the Duchess of Leinster, with her younger children and her sons' tutor, Mr Ogilvie, left Carton for Waterford, whence they embarked for France. Upon Mr Ogilvie's advice, the Duchess decided she could bring up the children with greater economy abroad.

Before leaving Ireland, the Duchess told William in confidence that she intended marrying Mr Ogilvie. He replied that, although he could not *wish* it, if it made her happy it was all he desired, and that she could not choose a person he had a better opinion of. The Duchess was married on 26 October, at Toulouse. The marriage caused a sensation in Irish and English social circles.

In 1775 William went to France, intending to pay a visit to his mother, who had taken a château near Marseilles. He got no further, however, than Paris, where he became ill. After a delay there of several weeks he gave up the attempt and returned to Ireland. But while in Paris William met the girl who was to become his wife; and it was not Miss FitzGerald. The young lady's name was Aemilia St George; she was seventeen years old, and was the only daughter and heiress of the last Lord St George. Her property, chiefly in Dublin and County Wicklow, brought in nearly 4,000 pounds a year.

She was exceedingly good-natured and agreeable. William became devoted to her, and she to him.

On 4 November, 1775, William, Duke of Leinster and Aemilia St George were married. After two days' honeymoon in County Wicklow, they took up their residence at Carton, which now belonged to William. Nothing could have been more Arcadian than William and Aemilia's life here. The young wife set out entirely to please her husband; the husband found that her good qualities surpassed anything he had imagined. In Carton itself and the demesne they enjoyed great happiness. 'I grow fonder of Carton every day', William declared. He improved the grounds; completing the widening of the Rye Water, making a new approach from the Kellystown gate, and lowering a portion of the the south-western side of the front lawn in order to have a view of the river from the hall door. With his horses, the chestnut colt, 'Sir Falstaff', and later, 'Crom-a-boo', he won races at the Curragh. In Dublin he entertained his friends at Leinster house. Masked balls were now being introduced into Dublin social life, a form of entertainment in which William delighted. At the masquerade at the Music Hall on the eve of St Patrick's Day,

---

* Caroline FitzGerald had married Robert King, Viscount Kingsborough, in 1769, shortly after William's return to Ireland from making his Grand Tour. One wonders whether William met her then, and what he thought of her. At any rate, her marriage turned out unhappily, and she and her husband were later separated.

1778, he appeared as an orange-girl, and created much enthusiasm by quickly changing his fruit for shamrocks as midnight chimed. At another fancy-dress ball at Leinster House, in order to encourage Irish industries, all the guests were dressed in materials of Irish manufacture, even the petticoats and the shoes of the ladies. On these occasions William received his guests at the head of the grand staircase, his manner being described as 'smooth and quiet'.

At Leinster House William finished the building and decorating of the picture gallery, so as to accomodate the large collection of pictures made by Lord St George, which his wife had brought into the family. He had the house painted and cleaned and papered; and with the spare pictures from the gallery he made 'the old blue drawing room a most beautiful room'. Wyatt sent him plans for the finishing of the picture gallery; which included an arched ceiling, highly enriched and painted. The gallery ran the whole depth of the house 70 feet by 24 feet wide; beneath it was the supper room, of the same dimensions, adorned with sixteen fluted Ionic columns, supporting a rich ceiling. Wyatt also prepared plans for alterations at Carton.

Beyond Leinster House Dublin was being built up. As early as 1775 William complained: 'They are building ... out at Leinster House, and what is more provoking is they are continuing Merrion Street and not the square'. When William's father had started to build Leinster House, then called Kildare House, in 1745 to the plans of Richard Castle, who, also designed Carton, the site chosen was Molesworth's Fields, then in the country. On the east side of the house was a garden and a lawn of considerable size; the upper windows commanded fine views of Dublin Bay.

At Carton, also, William received guests. Among these, in 1776, was Arthur Young. 'The park ranks among the finest in Ireland', he wrote; and went on to describe the demesne. He concludes by saying of William that 'Ireland is obliged to him for spending the revenue on the spot that produces it'. Young also mentions that William had built the town of Maynooth, which was regularly laid out and consisted of good houses; and that he encouraged people to settle there – 'consequently it increases'.

By October, 1776, Aemilia, 'the dear little Duchess', as William called his wife, was with child. 'The poor little soul is very sick, but otherways very well. I do so long for you to see her, you will doat on her. I believe she was made on purpose for me.' William and Aemilia were staying in Leinster House. Across the road, in Kildare Street, lived his grandmother, old Lady Kildare. She had lately been unwell, but this did not prevent her from paying her granddaughter-in-law a visit. 'Lady Kildare is very well, tho' still weak; she came here yesterday and would trot up to the Duchess's apartment, tho' I begged of her not, which tired her much. I think she is as cheerful and lively as ever'.

In December Aemilia's mother, Lady St George, stayed with her daughter and son-in-law at Carton. But William never cared for her. Indeed, he believed his wife's bad nerves had been caused by her having lived so much with her mother. Lady St George herself had not given up attempting to have children. 'She has had two miscarriages this year which has made her look younger,' observed William. 'Indeed, I believe she squeezes the poor things so that they could not go on in the natural progress, as she laces as tight as any opera dancer.'

In May, 1777, at Leinster House, the Duchess' first child was born. It was a girl. To William's delight 'there was no fuss, as it happened in the middle of the day, and no one but ourselves'. The midwife, little Mrs Lyons, arrived only just in time, having been delayed by another confinement. William's aunt, Lady Louisa Conolly, had been with them in the morning, went to Castletown during the day, and returned in the evening. William was glad to have Lady Louisa, who had promised to arrange everything about the nursing; for the Duchess was determined to nurse the child herself, against the wishes of doctors and nurses. Lady Kildare expressed the opinion that they would soon be tired of the trouble of nursing.

With the arrival of his child, William's happiness was complete. They returned to Carton, where he settled down to his farming. He also had his hunting, of which he was very fond. He possessed, he considered, 'the best pack of hare hounds perhaps in Europe'.

William's life was not spent entirely within the family circle. Although by temperament not attracted to the political world, he was through his rank and position drawn into public life. The war between England and France brought with it fears of a French invasion of both England and Ireland. As a defensive measure, the Volunteers were formed. William, Duke, was appointed Colonel of the First Dublin Regiment and General-in-Chief of the Volunteers. This was in 1779. But the defensive spirit of the Volunteers was soon changed. The American War had put ideas of liberty into every Irish head. If America was to become an independent nation, why not also Ireland? And what more suitable and convenient instrument could there be for the achievement of national independence than the

Volunteers? The force became the citizen army of 100,000 men.

The war, with its embargoes and restrictions, was paralysing Irish trade; in Dublin alone 19,000 weavers were out of work. Backed by armed strength, the Volunteers declared for Free Trade for Ireland. Enormous public enthusiasm was aroused; resolutions were passed; impressive reviews and great military parades were held. The appointment of William as General-in-Chief was celebrated with the greatest enthusiasm.

The ceremony took place on College Green, in front of Parliament House. Hundreds of people had collected there to watch the event. The Duke took his place at the head of the staff; before him, amid the salutes of the cannon and the shouts of the crowd, paraded all the local Volunteers – infantry, cavalry and artillery. The sight was so magnificent that strangers were led to believe that the people were crowning the Duke of Leinster King of Ireland!

A more ambitious man than William might indeed have attempted to place himself as the head of the nation, and rule all Ireland, as many of his ancestors had done before him. But, as we have already said, William was not by nature suited to politics. Added to which he was modest, loyal and conscientious; accustomed simply to take his place as the first gentleman of the land. In this capacity he had assumed the command of the great citizen army. Although his political views might be approved by his liberal cousin, Charles James Fox, his mild temper could not provide the leadership required by the progressives in Ireland. New men were called for; men with more insistent, determined voices; men who uttered louder and ever louder the cry, 'Free Trade for Ireland!' And so it came about that in July, 1780, it was not the Duke of Leinster but Lord Charlemont who was chosen to command the Volunteers. Grattan was appointed chief of staff. The American War continued to go badly for England. England's danger was Ireland's opportunity. In 1782 the Volunteers held a huge meeting at Dungannon and declared for a free Parliament. The force was a well-armed body of nearly 100,000 men, and could no longer be ignored. Neither could the intense feeling that had been aroused amongst the Irish people as a whole. The English Government – in which Charles Fox was Secretary of State – repealed the Act of George I: the Irish Parliament was free to legislate for itself. 'Spirit of Swift! Spirit of Molyneux! Your genius has prevailed', cried Grattan in a famous speech. 'Ireland is now a nation.' Eighteen years later Ireland's independence was again taken from her.

No longer in command of the Volunteers, William lived less and less in the public eye. Most of his time was spent at Carton. Here he entertained many distinguished people. Amongt those who stayed at Carton was Lady Caroline Dawson, afterwards Countess of Portarlington. Describing her visit, she tells how every morning the Duke's resident chaplain read prayers; how the Duchess appeared in a sack and hoop and diamonds in the afternoon; how French horns played at every meal; and how there were such quantities of plate and servants that one would imagine oneself to be in a palace. In the evening it was with the greatest difficulty that she could get anyone to play cards with her – William never liked this form of entertainment. The ladies sat and did needlework; the gentlemen lolloped about and went to sleep – William himself snoring so loudly on one occasion that everyone 'got into a great fit of laughing and waked him'.

In 1783 William was invested as the first Knight of St Patrick in Dublin Castle, the installation taking place in St Patrick's Cathedral. His stall in the chancel, above which are his name and his coat-of-arms, may still be seen. Also in 1783 William, with a brigade of Volunteers, was present on Leinster Lawn when Richard Crosbie ascended in his balloon in a vain attempt to fly to Wales.

In April 1787, William met with an accident which lamed him for life. He was at the theatre when some of the actors started fighting amongst themselves. The wife of one of them called out to the Duke to save her husband, whom she thought was being murdered. William leapt onto the stage, and in doing so fell upon the spikes, and remained there, with four wounds in his thigh, until lifted off. His recovery was slow. It was only when he was out of danger that news of the accident was broken to his wife, who was with child.

In 1789 William went to London as one of the Commissioners appointed to present the Irish Address to the Prince of Wales inviting him to become Regent during George III's madness. But the day on which William was received at Carlton House by the Prince, the King recovered; and William returned to Ireland. William paid for his friendship with the Prince by being deprived of the Mastership of the Rolls, an office to which he had been appointed the previous year. William remained a friend of the Prince of Wales; although he did not follow up an invitation from the future George IV to stay with him at Brighton – 'at my little Villa by the sea shore'.

By 1791 eight girls had been born to William and his Duchess. The birth of a son in August of that year caused much rejoicing. The

Dublin Volunteers assembled on Leinster Lawn and fired a *feu-de-joie*; at night many of the houses in the city were illuminated; the church bells were rung. The Prince of Wales was godfather to the child, who was given the names Augustus Frederick, those being two of the Prince's names. On the occasion of his christening, which took place at Carton, the Volunteers marched from Dublin, paraded in the courtyard, and enrolled the child in the company of Grenadiers. The little Marquis of Kildare grew up to be the third Duke of Leinster.

During the last decade of the century, there was much talk of Catholic emancipation in Ireland. Although William remained withdrawn from active political life, he expressed the opinion that this reform, long overdue, should now be carried through, but 'without shaking the foundation of the constitution'. But the recall of the well-intentioned Lord Fitzwilliam, after only 50 days in office as Lord-Lieutentant, put an end to all hope of Catholic emancipation and parliamentary reform.

The effects of the French Revolution on English and Irish opinion, causing the one to become reactionary, the other revolutionary, have been too often described to need repeating here. All that need be said is that for William living at Carton the situation became ever more complex. The Volunteer movement died down. Its place was now taken by a much more violent organisation – the 'Society of United Irishmen'. Formed in Belfast in 1791, it was led by Wolfe Tone. The headquarters of the Society were moved to Dublin. Its members declared a republic. Thenceforth they continued to work for an independent Ireland and they were obliged to work in secret.

From now on William's life became less happy. In 1796 his favourite brother, Lord Edward FitzGerald, joined the Society of United Irishmen. In April of that year he was one of two chosen by the Society to negotiate with the French for an invasion of Ireland. The threat to Ireland from the unsuccessful attempt of General Hoche's fleet to land in Bantry Bay caused the Government to introduce violent repressive measures. So barbarous were the outrages committed at the instigation of those in power that William raised his voice in protest. In addition, he resigned his civil and military appointments. He even went so far as to lend his brother considerable sums of money for the insurrectionary movement. It became known that he was giving every encouragement to the 'rebels'.

To add to William's unhappiness – his sorrow over his country's plight, his anxiety for his brother – his 'dear little Duchess' now became ill. In the autumn of 1797 they crossed to England and he took her to the Hot Wells at Bristol in the hopes that the change might be of benefit to her. But the state of her health did not improve and by the spring of 1798 he knew that she was dying.

Meanwhile a general rising had been secretly planned to take place at the end of May. It was to be led by Lord Edward himself. But now the plans for the insurrection were discovered by the Government spies, and the authorities, primed by an informer, swooped down upon the leaders of the rebellion. All, William learnt, had been arrested, with the exception of Lord Edward himself.

William was now very unhappy. His wife was desperately ill. His beloved brother, still organising the rebellion, was a fugitive with a price of £1,000 on his head. His Irish tenants were being subjected to political persecution. His friend, the Prince of Wales, condoled with him about his little Duchess, his brother and about the state of affairs in Ireland, which he considered were being horribly mismanaged.

In May William brought his wife to London. The elder children accompanied them. In May, too, William heard the news of Lord Edward's arrest in Dublin. He was told how his brother had been wounded while resisting arrest. He did not, however, realise the seriousness of the wound and was quite unprepared for the shock of his death which occurred in prison a fortnight later.

On 23 June William's 'dear little Duchess', Aemilia, died. She was only 39 years old.

William's sorrow was now complete. His married life had been one of great happiness. From the outset he and Aemilia had been devoted to each other. In his letters to his mother, William had never ceased to express his affection for his wife. 'The poor Duke of Leinster – how my heart bleeds for him!' wrote his aunt, Lady Sarah Napier. 'I am even now interrupted by the sad tidings of his last and still deeper misfortune being just at hand. God grant him fortitude! He has great feeling, little energy, and an accumulation of distress beyond the common lot of man. His lost brother, and the entire ruin of his fortune (perhaps for ever) are the preliminaries to his sorrows; deeply will he feel the loss ... His dear wife's attachment was of that nature never to be forgotten. She was his friend, his counsellor, with an uncommon share of sense and warmth of heart in all that concerned him, that made her the haven to which he looked in all his distresses. She soothed and calmed his griefs, pointed out remedies, and, by occupying him in his tender care of her sorrows, made him forget his own'.

William's affairs, already in a bad state, were brought to almost total ruin by the Rebellion. The county of Kildare, in which was all his property, was almost desolate, and growing worse every day. Terrible hardships were inflicted by the government on his tenants, and they were in no position to pay their rents.

The following year, 1799, William was back in Ireland. The question of Union was being discussed with much acrimony both in Ireland and in England. William steadfastly opposed the measure for the Union of Ireland with Great Britain from the moment it was first suggested. The Prince of Wales foresaw trouble ahead. He expressed his affection for William and all his family, and his great concern for their welfare. He urged the Duke to come over to England. 'Oh, for God's sake, my dear Duchess,' he said to William's mother, whom he met out driving in her coach, 'persuade him to come and be out of the way of all the disagreeable things that will be going on there; it would be the wisest step he could possibly take on many accounts to keep clear of it all'. In Parliament William consistently opposed and protested against the Union. In consequence, he was 'very justly *idolised* in Ireland'. But Pitt and the English Parliament were bent upon a Union. Forty-eight new peerages were created; £1,260,000 was spent on buying out the pocket boroughs.

From the unhappy state of Irish public affairs William took refuge at his beloved Carton. Here he was always contented. Although he no longer had his adored wife with him, to share his joys and disappointments, he was surrounded by his many children, to whom he was devoted. His happiness was increased when his eldest daughter, Mary, then in her early twenties, became engaged to Sir Charles Ross, a man of fine character, who was blessed with a fortune of £8,000 a year. They were married in 1799. William sent his two boys, Lord Kildare and Lord William FitzGerald, at the age of nine and eight years, respectively, to a school not far from Carton. With them he sent a letter to the headmaster of the school, the Reverend Gilbert Austin, expressing his wishes in regard to their upbringing. After saying he hoped Mr Austin would not find them much spoiled, and that their disposition was naturally good, and that care had been taken of their morals, he goes on to declare that he was not over anxious as to their being great scholars, 'as I think there are many more essential things for their future prospect in life. I wish their morals to be carefully attended to, and particular care to be taken that they should be taught upon all occasions to speak truth ...

They are naturally inclined to reading. I wish them to be perfect masters of history, particularly of their own country ... If anything should occur that you perceive any change in their manner or behaviour, you will let me know; for tho' they are upon a very familiar footing with me, yet I have great authority over them, tho' I scarce ever had occasion to be severe with them, the holding up of my finger was enough'.

In the year 1803 William spent some months in London. Soon after his return to Ireland Robert Emmet's insurrection broke out. It was easily suppressed. The Duke disapproved of the rising. Indeed, he advised the people not to join the rebellion, and persuaded them to give up their arms. In November of this same year William was again in London for the opening of Parliament; it was observed that he seemed in poor spirits and bad health. When he returned to Carton during the winter he was a very sick man.

William, second Duke of Leinster, died on 20 October 1804, at Carton, after six days' fever. He was in his fifty-fifth year. He was buried in St Bridget's Cathedral, Kildare. So well loved was he by all classes and all parties in Ireland that it was said the funeral procession stretched the whole length of the Curragh.

Various estimates of William's character were written after his death. All, including those of his political opponents, testify to his love of his country, his honesty in public life, and the affection in which he was held by his family and friends. He was, wrote Barringon, 'Generally respected as a public man, and universally beloved as a private one ... From the day of his maturity to the moment of his dissolution he was the undeviating friend of the Irish nation.' And in *The Gentleman's Magazine* the notice of his death contained the following words: 'He was not shining but good-tempered; good-natured and affable; a fond father, an indulgent landlord, and a kind master.'

BIBLIOGRAPHY

Doran, Dr, *'Mann' and Manners at the Court of Florence, 1740-1786*, Bentley (London), 1876.

Earl of Ilchester, *Henry Fox, 1st Lord Holland*, Murray (London), 1920.

FitzGerald, Brian (ed.), *Correspondence of Emily, Duchess of Leinster: 1731-1814*, Irish Mss. Comm. (Dublin), 1949.

FitzGerald, Brian, *Emily, Duchess of Leinster*, Staples (London), 1949.

Gooch, G.P., *Maria Theresa and Other Studies*, Longmans (London), 1951.

Jesse, J.H., *George Selwyn and his Contemporaries*, Nimmo (London), 1901.

Lambert, R.S., *Grand Tour*, Faber and Faber (London), 1935.

Maxwell, Constantia, *The English Traveller in France: 1698-1815*, Routledge (London), 1932.

Mead, W.E., *The Grand Tour in the Eighteenth Century*, Houghton Mifflin (Boston and New York), 1914.

More, Jasper, *The Land of Italy*, Batsford (London), 1949.

Russell, Lord John (ed.), *Memorials and Correspondence of C.J. Fox*, Bentley (London), 1853.

Sitwell, S., *German Baroque Art*, Duckworth (London), 1927.

Sitwell, S., *Southern Baroque Art*, Grant Richards (London), 1924.

Smolett, T., *Travels Through France and Italy*, Oxford University Press (World Classics), (London), 1907.

Trevelyan, Sir G.O., *Early History of C.J. Fox*, Longmans, Green (London), 1880.

Toynbee, Mrs Paget, *The Letters of Horace Walpole, Earl of Orford*, Clarendon Press (Oxford), 1903-25.

MORE FROM THIS PRESS

The Pleasing Hours

The Grand Tour of James Caulfeild, First Earl of Charlemont (1728-1799)

Cynthia O'Connor

The 1st Earl of Charlemont is best remembered today for having built the architectural masterpiece, the Casino at Marino, and Charlemont House, both in Dublin. He embarked on a Grand Tour from 1746 to 1754. In 1749 he sailed to Constantinople, Egypt, Asia Minor, the Greek islands and Greece. This voyage is historic in the annals of archaeology as he discovered the site of the lost city of Halicarnassus, the friezes from the Mausoleum of Bodrum and the description fizzles with excitement. He was founder of the Royal Irish Academy and became its first president in 1785.

1 898256 66 7 HB £20.00   1999

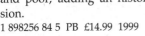

Bowen's Court

Elizabeth Bowen

Now back in print, this is the history of an Anglo-Irish family that arrived in north Cork as settlers in 1649. It is a classic history of the rise and fall of an Anglo-Irish family by one of this century's most highly regarded novelists and short-story writers. Throughout the book, Elizabeth's attachment to Bowen's Court, to tradition and to correct social behaviour are constant themes.

1 898256 44 6 PB £8.99   1998

Dress in Ireland

A History

Mairead Dunlevy

Traces the pattern of dress styles in Ireland from 750 BC using the earliest evidence of jewellery, clothes and shoes through the medieval era to the First World War. Photographs and illustrations depict both rich and poor, adding an historical/sociological dimension.

1 898256 84 5 PB £14.99 1999

White Knights, Dark Earls –

The Rise and Fall of an Anglo-Irish Dynasty
Bill Power

Foreword by William Trevor

The White Knights ruled vast estates in Munster until their long reign ended in the seventennth century when their land passed through marriage to the King family. In 1893 the third Earl of Kingston built Mitchelstown Castle, the largest in Ireland. But trouble followed trouble. In August 1922 Republican forces burned the castle. This is the story of an extraordinarily powerful dynasty that echoes Ireland's history.

1-898256-94-2 PB £14.99 2000

Surplus People

The Fitzwilliam Clearances 1847-1856
Jim Rees

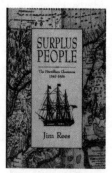

From 1847 to 1856, Lord Fitzwilliam arranged 'assisted passages' to Canada for 6,000 men, women and children from his 80,000-acre Coolattin estate in Wicklow. Most were destitute on arrival in Quebec and New Brunswick. Despite good intentions there was terrible misunderstanding. This book describes the clearances and examines how some of the families fared in Canada. It also focuses on the infamous Grosse Île near Quebec.

1-898256-93-4 PB £9.99 2000

Fairy legends and Traditions of Ireland
Thomas Crofton Croker

First published in 1825 and sold out in a week, this reprint was issued to celebrate the 200th anniversary of the birth of the author. Croker roamed the countryside collecting tales and lore from peasants and storytellers. The lively wit of the peasants, the wild energies of nature, the poverty, the struggle to make ends meet, all can be detected under the surface of the printed words. The brothers Grimm translated the book into German.

1-898256-53-5 PB £7.99 1998